Investing For Beginners

Quickstart Guide On Stock Market, Forex Trading, Futures, Etfs And Cryptocurrency

(Transform Your Life And Get Rich With Early Retirement)

Magnus Brewer

Published By **John Kembrey**

Magnus Brewer

All Rights Reserved

Investing For Beginners: Quickstart Guide On Stock Market, Forex Trading, Futures, Etfs And Cryptocurrency (Transform Your Life And Get Rich With Early Retirement)

ISBN 978-1-77485-845-5

All rights reserved. No part of this guidebook shall be reproduced in any form without permission in writing from the publisher except in the case of brief quotations embodied in critical articles or reviews.

Legal & Disclaimer

The information contained in this ebook is not designed to replace or take the place of any form of medicine or professional medical advice. The information in this ebook has been provided for educational & entertainment purposes only.

The information contained in this book has been compiled from sources deemed reliable, and it is accurate to the best of the Author's knowledge; however, the Author cannot guarantee its accuracy and validity and cannot be held liable for any errors or omissions. Changes are periodically made to this book. You must consult your doctor or get professional medical advice before using any of the suggested remedies, techniques, or information in this book.

Upon using the information contained in this book, you agree to hold harmless the Author from and against any damages, costs, and expenses, including any legal fees potentially resulting from the application of any of the information provided by this guide. This disclaimer applies to any damages or injury caused by the use and application, whether directly or indirectly, of any advice or information presented, whether for breach of contract, tort, negligence, personal injury, criminal intent, or under any other cause of action.

You agree to accept all risks of using the information presented inside this book. You need to consult a professional medical practitioner in order to ensure you are both able and healthy enough to participate in this program.

Table of Contents

Chapter 1: Taking Control Of Your Finances 1

Chapter 2: Risk And Return 16

Chapter 3: Importance And Importance Of Financial Investment 31

Chapter 4: The Good, The Bad, And The Ugly Investments 37

Chapter 5: Drop Shipping 49

Chapter 6: 11 Proven Investment Strategies That Work For A Small Amount Of Money 64

Chapter 7: Choosing Stocks To Invest In. 71

Chapter 8: Risk Tolerance 81

Chapter 9: Habits Of Investment - The Beginner's Stage 91

Chapter 10: Swing-Trading Stocks 100

Chapter 11: Market Volatility & Market Expectation 118

Chapter 12: Socially Conscious Investments And The Law Of Abundance 124

Chapter 13: Advantages Of Index Funds 146

Chapter 14: Scalping Guide 162

Chapter 15: Retaining And Managing Your Tenants 170

Conclusion 184

Chapter 1: Taking Control Of Your Finances

We don't always see how much we could be sabotaging the finances of our families. Sometimes, we might think we're doing the right and end up making a wrong decision that could lead to real money that actually makes sense. If we are too focused on other people's success and do not look out for our own financial stability we may lose money more quickly than we make. Money is not everything. And we shouldn't be constantly thinking about it. It is possible to have a steady income without worrying about where the next paycheck is coming. Learning how to manage our money effectively will allow us to make more without having the same amount of effort as in the actual "labor" portion.

The first step in creating a budget is to make it. This is how much you are able to spend each week or month. It does not matter if you make a regular salary or your income is fluctuating from week-to-week. The first step in determining your weekly average in money coming in is to take taxes into consideration. Most people get taxes taken out from their wages. But, there are some individuals who have to file income separately and pay taxes later. Once taxes have been determined, it's time to consider how much money should go towards utilities. It is important to make sure that you are earning twice as much each month than it takes to pay for all your monthly necessities. That includes rent or mortgage, electricity, internet/cables, water, waste and gas, credit card payments, or any other fees or charges we need to be aware of. Rest money is money that goes to the essential functions of daily living such as food, clothing, and toiletries. Both utility and function must be reduced in order to preserve some amount for savings.

Budgeting can be as simple as setting realistic goals. Budgeting is difficult if you don't have the ability to save half your monthly income. Sometimes, our goals sound too lofty and are almost impossible to attain. This is because we fantasize about the outcome rather than taking responsibility for actual achieving those goals. We set ourselves up for failure if we have unrealistic goals. This leads to disappointment which then leads to depression and lack of motivation. It can be hard to keep trying if you feel like you're failing. It is essential to realize that setting realistic goals and being practical about them will help us avoid putting ourselves in a negative situation.

You should look at how much money you are spending on food. It could be as easy as cutting back on your grocery bill. Do you eat out more than you cook at the home? Do you prefer to buy fast food over making meals that can last you for the whole week? Make sure you eat meals that are made from food you purchased at the grocery store more often then you eat at a restaurant. Eating out is more appealing because you can enjoy a meal made by someone else.

Build Your Path to Investing

Investing allows you to grow your income. You can save enough money, pay your bills, and then put the money toward a project which could potentially double your income. You can either invest in a large or smaller amount. No matter what your choice, it's possible to make more money by investing with the cash you have left.

This could be a side hustle, or it could eventually become your main income source. It might be possible to invest $500 per month in something that offers a high return. You'll soon be earning $16,000 within five years of your investment if it doubles every month. While this may not be true for every company, it is a great way to leverage the cash you already have and make it even more.

It is income which helps plan for the long-term. You don't buy anything if you have an investment. An investment is more about setting yourself up for the future. By being able look ahead six, twelve, and 24 years, you'll be better able to manage your finances.

The goal is eventually to have enough investment to not have to worry any more about employment.

There are many options for investing. You might choose to invest in yourself, or use your talents and skills. You may know someone who's looking to invest, or maybe you are connected with an existing business online. You could also invest in real estate or stocks, which are both lucrative and likely to continue being around for some time.

Investing in retirement will also help with taxes. You may get tax breaks for making an investment depending on the type. However, once you start spending the money, you won't need to worry about any tax. You don't have to tax your money on the year it was earned. Instead, you pay tax when you die.

The money does the work. It doesn't matter if you have to go to work every day or work for minimal wages. You can be in control of your own money. We have been working for people who pay us little while they make the most money. Now it's our turn to earn all the money ourselves without having to follow someone else's rules.

It creates passive income. It's possible to make money from real estate investments without having to do any work. If you are unable to perform the work required to get the position, you can hire someone who will do it for you. You can now make your own money, without having to clock in at work.

It serves as a protection blanket. Your investments can serve as reminders that more money is coming in. You shouldn't be afraid of making investments that are risky. However, you can make sure your money goes towards smart investments. Some people like the risk that comes with higher investments. Many people have the patience to be safe and make their money last longer.

Cut the unnecessary

It is important to review what you are spending money on, and eliminate it from your budget. There are many expenses in our lives that we don't often realize are completely unnecessary. Some people don't stop to think about the things they spend their money on, and how much they can save if they cut out those costs completely. Others spend mindlessly, wondering where their money goes. They don't stop to think about the things that they buy, even if they are totally unnecessary.

Think about how you use transportation. Do you own a car that can take you to work or school? There are people who live in areas where cars may be absolutely essential, while others prefer to use public transportation, even though it can cost them more. To save money on fuel, tolls, and parking, you should reduce your car's usage. Driving to work every day means you're paying a parking fee. Consider whether the car you currently have is right for you. Some people feel the urge to buy more expensive cars and larger vehicles.

Internet and cable can be very expensive, which is why we don't often use them. Is it really worth spending over $100 each month just to have one channel that you regularly watch? Netflix, Hulu or HBO go are streaming services that offer many options to choose from. This is in contrast to cable which can be cluttered with advertisements and slow with the content it actually provides. It doesn't matter if you are only using cable to watch a certain channel. You might be able to just view the DVD or Blu-ray once and not have to pay for it again. These two things can really lighten your burden if you lower your weekly costs.

Bad habits can lead you to paying unnecessary prices. How you shop can impact your spending habits. Think about how you shop. Do you have a plan? Or are you more dependent on looking at the sale or seeing what you like? You will spend more than you intend to and buy unnecessary products that you just don't need.

There are always ways to save money. Even if you barely make it, there is always something you can do that will save you money. Perhaps it's a cup or two of morning coffee each day, or just buying icecream every time you go grocery shopping. If you save just $5 per week, you can have $260 at your end of the fiscal year. This may seem small, but imagine that you could double your investment each year to make $260. If your investment increases by %200 per year over 10 years, it could make you an investment worth $100,000.

Sometimes it is necessary to consolidate different expenses in order to save money. Even though you might pay more than your minimum payment but you have all bills in order, this doesn't mean you're being as efficient as you can with your finances. You may still have room for improvement.

Consolidate

Consolidation is a term that people associate with someone who takes out loans to pay off multiple credit cards simultaneously. You can then make one monthly loan payment. This is one kind of consolidation. It can still be quite helpful to do this. Instead, making five $50 payments on credit card accounts with different interest rates you can instead pay $200 per month on a loan which has a lower rate of interest than all credit cards. This option is definitely worth looking into if you are able. Consolidating your company is possible in several other ways.

You may be able consolidate your retirement account. You should make sure you're financially stable before doing this. Sometimes, our retirement funds are just sitting there. It might not be earning the same interest rate as our credit card debt. So, if your credit scores are increasing 20% annually and you have $10,000 worth of credit card debt you can expect to build up debt. Maybe you have a retirement savings fund with $35,000. Then, maybe you have a retirement plan that has $35,000.

Other ways to consolidate are available. This may be found in the other bills that are being paid. Is it possible to bundle multiple services that you already pay for? Do you think you could combine some services to get more value? You might be thinking about your cell phone bills, or your internet service. Find other people to share your responsibilities, even though they may not live near you. Trustworthiness is a must. You could save money if you combine your payments.

You should think about your beauty habits. Think about your beauty habits. Do you need to buy new makeup every week? Or do you just have to get your nails done more often than necessary? Maybe your haircuts are too costly. And what about the way your dog is groomed? Although we feel pressure to keep up our beauty standards, it doesn't necessarily mean that we will stop spending on costly treatments. Sometimes it's enough to simply look at the vanity side of things to save a few bucks.

You can consolidate spending on other areas of your life. Instead of spending money on food and grocery shopping twice a week, shop at Sam's Club or Costco to get bulk items. To resist temptation, it is easier to stay away from the supermarket and stick to a meal plan that is cost-effective.

All of these methods will help you become a better investor. Save money and you will have more money for investing. Instead of spending $20 to buy a meal, which you may forget about, you could put that $20 towards $200 investments that will double over time and earn you a lot of extra money. Even though it may be hard to say no, it is the best way of saving money.

Ten Percent Off Your Income

Saving for your future is vital. It's fun to spend right now but it's better to save for the future. The society we live in seems to make saving less important. Many people prefer to go into massive, potentially dangerous debt rather than thinking about setting up a retirement account. Because retirement is important, we shouldn't need to work until we die. Many people think they will be able to work, but others believe they won't. Retirement isn't right for everyone. However, there are times when we have to leave work due to our health. As we get older, major body parts like our hips or backs are more likely to be broken. An injury like this can leave us without work at 70 and beyond. Our risk of getting heart or lung disease, as well as mind-altering illnesses like Alzheimer's or dementia, is higher. These things can happen despite our best efforts. While you might not want the decision to retire, it's important to save money for an illness or emergency that may affect your ability work.

You might not be using 90% of the basic items you need to get by. It's possible to save more than 10 per cent by consolidating and cutting expenses. This amount should go straight to a retirement fund. While many people have retirement funds that are set up by their employers, it's better to have your own.

You will have more money later if your lifestyle isn't one of the above. Even though you may have the means to purchase luxury items in your life, there is no reason to be extravagant. Is it possible to find more affordable ways of living and save money that you can use later?

Did you ever feel the thrill of finding an old $10 bill or $2o in your winter coat pocket. Imagine reaching 80 years old and discovering that you have more $200,000 left for whatever you desire. Retirement can also be scary for many. People fear the idea of becoming old, sick or dying. It's not scary if you approach it that way. If you ensure that you have the funds to support this stage of life, you will feel less anxious about what lies ahead.

Sometimes, it might be necessary to aim for higher than 10 percent. If you desire to live a luxurious lifestyle, and you plan to continue it in the future you will want to set yourself up for more than 10 percent.

The less you have to save the sooner you get started. It's okay to not save enough for every month. Don't be afraid to give more money than 10% every paycheck. However, if you don't have the means, it's OK. Sometimes we have the need to pay more for different costs. So we shouldn't be too hard on ourselves for not being consistent.

Section off savings when you have more income. If you don't have enough income, save 25 percent for retirement. 10 percent will go to an emergency fund. 15 percent will go towards a specific fund that you invest in. Now that you're aware of the potential benefits that investing can bring to you now, and into the future, you can look at the options available for you to invest.

Chapter 2: Risk And Return

The investment world is very aware of the importance and necessity of understanding the concepts risk, return, diversification, portfolio building, and diversification. This chapter will give you a thorough explanation of each and provide steps to create a diversification portfolio.

Risk and returns in the world of investment

Investors face many risks when they invest in the financial world. Investors face many risks in the world of investment. Some are very serious and can have long-term consequences. Some are just human biases and feelings. If the organization that you are investing in goes bankrupt, this is a type of risk. It means that you could lose money. This does not have to happen often and the risks can be mitigated by diversification. Diversification is also a good idea, as it doesn't guarantee high returns.

Diversification is a way to reduce risk. Managers and investment advisers will often speak of currency, interest rate, and market risks. Each one can cause profits or returns to be lower than expected and in some cases even negative. But they can all be managed and are part of larger risks.

This happens when investors are too conservative or inexperienced. You will face unpredicted risks that could have a negative effect on your assets. New Zealand's foot diseases are an example.

However, there are some principles you can use to manage risk.

There are always risks. The returns are only one half of the equation. Short-term risk is often greater for those earning higher long-term earnings than they are for the short-term. Investors who take responsibility for managing these risks and do not seek to eliminate risk are the ones that reap the rewards. The other side of investment is risk. It is crucial that you understand the risks involved in the investment you are making and how they will affect your financial goals.

Understanding risks and ensuring transparency about returns are essential. Investment risks that are not fully understood can make it difficult to manage. Returns'sources' are not transparent. This increases the risk of being unaware. It is important to first understand the basics of investing and then use common sense.

Experience and judgement are key. It is impossible to manage risks with mathematical models or ratios. An investor may use a risk-reward tool to determine the expected returns and risk to obtain these returns. They serve as a basis for making the right judgement.

Diversification. This will be discussed in greater detail in the next section. Diversification can be described as multiple investments within one asset class. It reduces risk while not changing the expected returns.

Diversification lowers uncertainty so that the return outcome is often different.

Consistency. A consistent, steady approach to managing risk will be better than a dynamic process. It provides a framework that allows for better understanding the final result. It is crucial to know where competitive advantage can be found, and how decisions can be made on that basis.

Diversification and portfolio building concepts

It is tempting to check the investment value in certain situations. But even experienced investors will find that emotions can sometimes stop them from evaluating their investments. You need to review your portfolio regularly, at most once per day. If your financial condition changes significantly, you will also need to do so. When you lose your job or are awarded a significant bonus. You will be a long-term success if you have a strategic asset share.

Diversify to make money

Diversification can't be used to guarantee profits or losses, but it can improve performance. But diversification, if you focus on a risk level that is appropriate for your objectives and accept volatility, can increase the chances of maximizing returns. A diversified portfolio is possible by searching for assets and investments that didn't perform in the exact same way. So, if one portion of your portfolio is not performing well, you can grow the other part. By doing this, you can offset poor performance and avoid it from negatively impacting the portfolio. It is important to keep your portfolio diverse across investment types. Make sure that you don't over concentrate on any one stock in your stocks. A stock that is worth less than 5% of your overall stock holdings could be a problem.

Diversification has proved to be a successful strategy

Diverse investment options suffered considerable losses in 2008's bear market.

Diversification didn't fail, even though it looked like it. The most important asset classes were actually more related, so diversification still helped to prevent portfolio losses from buy-and hold. Three hypothetical portfolios are considered: a portfolio with 70% stocks and 25% of short term investments. Finally, a portfolio with 25% bonds.

Diversification allowed for the reduction of losses and preservation of gains during the financial crisis

Source: Strategic Advisers, Inc.

The asset's hypothetical worth was maintained in untaxed accounts of $100,000 in cash portfolios. This portfolio is diversified and includes 49% U.S. Stocks and 21% Global Stocks. Both stocks as well as the diversified portfolio saw a decline by February 2009. But, they lost half of what they were worth at the beginning. The diversified portfolio however lost more than one third of their initial value. Even though losses could have been lower in a diversified portfolio, diversification would have contributed to fewer losses than an all-stock portfolio.

Investors get lower returns than some indexes in this market

January 2004, December 2014

Source: Quantitative Analysis of investor Behavior (QAIB), 2015

A diversified portfolio and stocks will decrease when investors are faced with stressful situations. This can sometimes lead to short-term, quick decisions like selling stocks. Yes, in February 2009 it might have seemed like a good idea to keep cash. Take a look at the events that took place when the market became stable again.

After being at the bottom for five years, our all-stock portfolio would now have grown by 162.3%. Our diversification portfolio would also have increased by around 99.7%. All stock portfolios benefit the most from the market's upswing. This is a good example of how portfolios may gain less than all stock portfolios and a lot greater than portfolios that are entirely cash. Let's examine what happened over a longer span of time. In the time period from January 2008 to February 2014, portfolios that were diversified increased by 29.9% and portfolios that were all-stock increased by 31.8%. This is the core purpose of diversification. Although it doesn't necessarily improve profits in rising stock markets, it captures many opportunities while being more volatile than investing directly in stocks.

Bad timing comes at a high price

Why is it so important to accept a certain level of risk? The chart above shows how diversification can lead to a portfolio that plays over time. Many investors don't realize the potential benefits of their investment strategies. This is why they often pursue higher-risk investments and go after performance.

Investors will often opt for less risk investments when there are market problems. These decisions can mean missed opportunities during market recovery. These investors are notorious for underperforming in bear markets. Research has repeatedly shown that while average stocks and bonds can generate returns, returns from fund investors fall by large margins. Reports of returns and profits for average stocks are also consistent with this conclusion.

Research by DALBAR reveals that fund investors often follow markets. Diversification decisions that they make generate lower returns for overall markets. Investors can overcome these problems if they have a well-thought out plan. This plan should include the proper investment mix and rebalancing.

How to build a portfolio that is diverse

It is important to align your investment portfolio with your investment goals, financial objectives, and level of volatility. The past performance of your investment vehicles and future results is no guarantee. The only way to earn returns is to reinvest dividends and other types earnings. But diversification doesn't happen overnight. Investments can change over time. The chart below illustrates the difference in performance between diversification portfolios for 1995 and 2015.

Data Source: Ibbotson Associates, 2015 (1926-2014).

This chart illustrates monthly performance from 1995 to 2015. Stocks can be demonstrated using the S&P 500 index, while bonds can be demonstrated using Barclays intermediate Treasury bonds indexes. Finally, the U.S. 30-day T.bills can be used to show short-term investments. A target mix is something you should keep in mind. You need to check and reevaluate your portfolio regularly. You can make your portfolio more risky if you don't regularly reevaluate.

What happens when your portfolio isn't balanced? Let's consider a portfolio we have built over a twenty year period. This will demonstrate how market changes, such as the S&P 500 rise, can impact portfolio investment mix and risk levels. Let's say that the portfolio experienced a growth of 80% stocks, 10% bonds, and 10% short term investments between April 1995 and April 1995. Twenty years later, the mix is completely different and all its components are experiencing an increase.

Important to note is that past performance doesn't always guarantee profitability, especially when stocks have experienced greater cost swings than money and bonds. Portfolios tilting towards stocks can lead to bigger increases. Due to changes in assets allocation relative to investment vehicles, portfolio risk was 10% higher that target mixes. The portfolio's risk is assessed using the yearly standard deviation in monthly returns. This demonstrates the volatility of returns.

Let's look at these risk levels over time. We will use two scenarios as an illustration. If investment mixes are rebalanced on a regular basis back to target, and if no revaluations have taken place (a purchase & hold technique). Portfolios that are purchase-and-hold have different risk levels than those that are rebalanced. This portfolio has higher risks, resulting in greater portfolio volatility. Rebalancing and reviewing your portfolio is not a way to lower risk. The goal is to rebalance your investment mix in a manner that reduces risk. Sometimes this means reducing risk levels by increasing portfolio portion in conservative choices. However, it can increase risk and make it difficult to get back at the target mix. This could mean that you increase your investment in more risky assets like stocks. It is necessary to establish a strategy, pick the best investment and conduct regular checks to ensure your portfolio remains on track. These three steps will help you get there:

I)Know the best investment mix.

(April 1995-March 2015)

Source: Quantitative Analysis of investor Behavior (QAIB 2015).

The chart shown above is for demonstrational purposes only. This chart illustrates historical risk associated with the performance of diversifiedindices. Portfolios without diversification can experience different levels of risk.

If you have not already done this, you should choose the investment vehicle that is most suitable for your investment goals and objectives. Consider your finances, levels of volatility and how much money you are going to need. You should consider how long you have to invest. The higher the number of investment vehicles in your portfolio, the better. Stocks are a good example of this. However, they have greater growth potential, and the time frame can help reduce volatility. It is worth looking at investments that are less volatile such as bonds or short-term investments if you have a need for the money in the near future. By doing this, you can trade more volatility for greater returns.

II) Examine your portfolio on a regular basis

It is recommended to monitor your investment portfolio on a yearly basis. Rebalancing your portfolio is essential to address any significant changes that may have an impact on it. You should consider rebalancing if your stock allocation is moving away from the target 10%.

III) Rebalancing your portfolio

There are many options to rebalance your portfolio. One way is to sell asset classes that you aren't using and then reinvest those gains in the ones that are more within your target. Selling securities that are taxable can have different tax consequences. It is crucial to factor taxes into your decision when buying or selling securities. Rebalancing your portfolio without immediate tax results is another way to do it. This involves investing the money slowly or simultaneously.

No matter which approach you take, the most important aspect of rebalancing your portfolio is to keep it diverse in all investment types. To achieve your long-term goals, you must balance risks and rewards. Monitoring your investments can make a significant difference to your long-term success.

Chapter 3: Importance And Importance Of Financial Investment

How can wealthy people build their fortunes through these methods? What are the key factors that allow wealthy people to make such large returns? The conventional wisdom is that more wealthy individuals should allocate more of their assets to high risk investments in order to get higher returns. However, our study found that even though they make better choices, rich people often get a higher rate of return on their assets. Wealthy individuals get "returns on scale" from their investments. To be more precise, people who are financially well-off are more likely achieve higher risk-adjusted portfolio returns. This may be due to having access to superior wealth managers or unique investment options. It is important to take into account financial intelligence, financial literacy, and entrepreneurial skills. These characteristics ensure that the returns to wealth are constant over time. This research is unique in that it quantifies this process and shows its relevance for economics.

Can high returns be sustained over time? The qualified answer to this question is yes. Wealth is highly intergenerational. However, there are significant differences in how the different generations receive their wealth. Even though the wealthiest individuals are likely to have their children very rich, it is unlikely that they will receive the same returns on their investments as their parents. This proves that even the most skilled people cannot pass down wealth. However, money may be passed down without any problems.

They also tend toward similar wealth-building techniques such as saving as many as they can and creating several streams of income. Millionaires prefer to invest in low-cost real estate and index funds over other types of investment. Millionaires are also more likely than average people to be financially responsible, diligent, and resilient - all of which can aid in increasing their wealth.

These behaviors are also possible in non millionaires. Millionaires however, tend to exhibit them more often and more consistently.

Millionaires reap the benefits of frugality. It is a commitment towards saving money, spending less and adhering strictly to a financial plan. Frugality contributes to their success. Spending beyond what you can afford and not saving enough for retirement will make you a slave your income. Millionaires can save money on their expenses by being thrifty and purchasing a reasonable-priced property. They recognize that their income does not suffice and have to set aside some.

Although the savings rate might not be accurate due to factors such tax avoidance, the core point is that millionaires actually save more than the average person.

Federal Reserve estimates that you will be no worse off if your annual income is $250,000 and your annual expenditures are $250,000.

Mindset difference between rich and poor

The stark differences in mindsets between the rich and the poor are illustrated here.

This isn't about a race between the wealthy and the needy. Many poor people may have a positive outlook but are financially poor due to their circumstances. Many trust fund infants are negative in outlook.

Wealthy people know that first, they must accumulate a lot of wealth. Next, put that wealth to use to speed things up. Education should not be delayed. Increase the efficiency of a company's operations. Accelerate the next generation.

An unhappy consumer will immediately see a surplus in excess as an opportunity to buy.

A wealthy mentality is one that seeks to invest their money, time, and energy into activities that will continue to provide income long after the initial investment is made. It is important to have a wealth mindset. You need to be able to drive the needle and create urgency. Once systems are in place, they will produce value.

Bad attitudes will only bring short-term benefits. Hours-for-dollars. Resource that does not immediately yield a return on investment are called squandered.

A wealthy mindset will be willing to invest resources even if it does not provide immediate benefit.

If someone is feeling down, "What's the point in it for me?" is often the first thing that pops into your head. You don't get paid to travel to conferences, to pay for hotel rooms, or to spend your free time. The goal of the rich mentality seeks to create trusting connections, such as mutual respect and shared values. The wealthy attitude encourages people to be generous and help others without expecting anything in return.

"I scratch your head, you scratch mine," says someone with a bad attitude.

A wealthy mindset knows that trust is earned slowly through hard-fought, bleeding labor. Reputation can be damaged in an instant.

A poor attitude can lead to them sacrificing their reputation for quick cash. If you have a broad perspective, you are able to accept that reality is not fair. You also know how to deal with it respectfully and practical. It recognizes that it is not owed anything by this world, that the cosmos doesn't care about its existence, or that life is a series of painful and unsustainable states. All triumphs are unlikely. They should be recognized as such when they happen.

A poor attitude is one that makes you irritable about the world's inequalities and you spend most of your time complaining. It believes the entire world owes its something, and it patiently waits for that something.

Chapter 4: The Good, The Bad, And The Ugly Investments

While investing money can be very rewarding, it can also be complicated. It means that you are willing to put your money into something with the hopes of getting a great financial return. Although you're saving your money by investing, you'll reap the rewards more if you put in the time and effort to invest.

If you are willing to put in the work, investing can be a good way for you to make money. Be aware that every investment comes with risk. As you move past the beginner stage, be aware of your risks and be smart. You will need to have patience and do a lot research before you can make money from investments.

This can be a great way to invest in real estate if you know the differences. Multi-property real estate investments can be a great way of making a large income. Renting out multiple properties to make an income is an option.

However, you have the option to either buy them all or fix them up and make a good profit.

You have many options to use real estate investments to make a big profit.

Renting properties: This is an excellent way to make money. You buy a home, make sure it is attractive to potential renters, then collect rent from them. Short term and long-term rentals are also possible. You are responsible to fix any issues in your home and maintain the repairs.

Airbnb: Airbnb is available for short-term tenants to rent out.

Buy and hold: This means you buy a home and keep it for as long as the market is up. After that, you can either sell it at higher prices or make a nice profit. This strategy is longer term, however.

Fix and flip is a popular way for people to make extra money. However it can be very time-consuming as you have to purchase the property, fix it up and then move on to the next step. This will require you to hire a team that can help with things like electric and plumbing.

Real estate investment Trust (REIT: This is a much simpler investment than the others. It works almost as if you were investing in stock or shares. Your investment will then flourish.

If you are like most, you may have reasons not to purchase a property. Maybe you don't have enough to save for a deposit. Some people prefer renting to save money and avoid the hassle of keeping a house in good condition. You can rent a home, suit, bouncy house or robot kitchen, regardless of the reason.

You must have a valid lease written by all parties. It should include all terms and requirements.

Make sure to find out the date that rent is due. Also, make sure you are aware of the penalties for late payments.

It is important to read the policies for pets and understand any extra charges. Usually, they will charge half of your rent.

It is important to find out whether you are responsible for snow or grass removal.

The deposit you pay will cover any damage you may cause while you live there. Be sure to understand the meaning of that term. Some things, such as hanging pictures and drilling holes in walls, can be considered normal wear and tear depending on the length and duration of the lease agreement.

You must ensure that you fully understand the rules of noise in your lease agreement.

Any other terms you may have, such as what is and what isn't allowed on the deck, if any.

Stocks and Bonds

What are stocks?

Stocks are an investment type where you can choose to invest in the company you see listed on the stock market. In other words, you can purchase a small amount of the company. Stocks can be tricky as they can move up and down, or vice versa. Diversifying your investments is important. You will be worse off if your investments aren't in multiple companies. Before you invest, make sure to find out what fees may apply. It is simple to access the information via an online investment platform.

Let's look at diversification. Diversification involves spreading your investments among different types companies. There's less risk of losing a large amount of money. It's the old saying, "Don't put all your eggs into one basket." If one of you investments isn't performing well, don't lose everything. Maybe another company is doing better.

What are bonds?

Bonds are a type of loan that must be paid back by the borrower. There are corporate bonds as well as government bonds. They are less risky that stocks. As you are lending money, the company or organization is lending it to you. The lender pays back the amount once the bond matures.

A return on investment is what the bond industry calls it. This is how much you receive back relative to what your put in. This could be money you invest in your company or your own time. This is not the equivalent of profit. It is where your expenses exceed your income. ROE can help your business determine if the work you do is beneficial or unnecessary. Your total cost is divided by your net benefits to calculate ROE.

Let's now get to the point: liquidity. Liquidity can be defined as the ability of capital (assets you have) to be converted to cash. It does not affect its market value.

You should continue your education even after you've graduated from high school. It is vital for your future career. The sooner you begin to save money, the greater. A Registered Education Savings Plan (or RESP) is something you can open. A registered education savings plan is what this means.

This is a great option to have money in a separate account so it is not easy to spend or get to. The best part about an RESP is that you get government assistance by contributing.

An RRSP is a registered retirement savings program. It is vital to be aware of it for your future. It has been around over 60 year! You can get one set up and be assured of having something in your savings for when you retire. Most people retire between the ages of 60-60. Some jobs offer retirement savings, but it's important to make sure you have your own. The best thing about an RRSP? You can add a certain amount. This amount is taken from your earned income. If you earn $60,000 and contribute $8,200 each year, the government will pretend that you made only $51,800 when you file for taxes (Goldman, 202).

Always remember that investing comes with risk. The ratio of high/low risk/reward reflects the level of risk that you are taking with your investments and the type of return or reward you will get. This would be profit divided with loss. It is important you understand how much risk you are willing to take on each trade.

There are some investments you should avoid. These investments are not worth your time.

Timeshare: If you purchase a property in time, this is where you share the ownership of the property for a year. It won't be worth the money you invest.

Restaurants: It takes a lot to keep a restaurant thriving and open. A restaurant must also be able to hire competent staff.

Penny Stocks: These stocks can be very inexpensive and believed to be the next big thing. However, they aren't properly regulated and difficult to trade.

You should not invest in anything that you don't understand. Do extensive research about the company's history and background.

Cryptocurrency

Cryptocurrency is often mentioned. It is a digital currency that can be used to pay online for goods and services. There are more than 10,000 types. They can be used as tokens in companies, and traded for specific goods or services.

Cryptocurrency makes use of a technology known as blockchain. It helps keep transactions online secure and allows for the management and tracking of transactions. Everyone wants to buy some crypto before it becomes even more valuable. People like that the bank is less involved in managing their funds.

So, the question is: are they a good idea or a bad investment? Just like real currency, cryptocurrencies don't generate cash flow. Therefore, in order to make any profit, someone must pay more for the currency that you paid. Many people find the idea unstable.

Online wallets are required in order to purchase cryptocurrency. This allows you to transfer money real money to purchase cryptocurrency. Are they legal Yes and no. They are legal, but some countries have banned their use.

This is an opportunity for scammers to take advantage of you and make money. You can be smart and secure yourself.

Bitcoin is the most used cryptocurrency.

Why is bitcoin so beloved? To everyone's delight, the bitcoin value has skyrocketed several times in the past and is still climbing. The value of many other cryptocurrency types is rising and everyone wants to get a piece. Bitcoin was created by Satoshi Nakamoto in 2018. It was anonymously created by a group of people.

This currency has huge potential. Because it offers many user-friendly perks, it is extremely popular. It is self-sustainable and offers anonymity.

Meet Jaydyn Carr

Jaydyn Carr, a San Antonio boy aged ten, made some smart investments and cashed his profits from his smart money decisions. Jaydyn got ten GameStop share certificates from his mother back in 2019. Each one cost $6.19. GameStop is an online video game company. His mother bought shares in GameStop because her son loved the games. His stake of $60 grew quickly and he now owns $3,200. Jaydyn learned everything about the stock exchange from Jaydyn's mom. He made the wise decision to sell the stock and keep the money. There was always the possibility that he might lose it all. Jaydyn made the decision to keep $1,000 of his earnings to help his mother invest, and to deposit the remainder in a savings account.

This story proves that you never know what might happen to your money. Being wise about how you save it will allow you to appreciate the value of money and teach you how money management works. How cool it is to own a little of your favorite business!

Chapter 5: Drop Shipping

What is drop shipping?

Is it possible to own a business selling or supplying products you don't possess? Can you also invest with no physical location?

Drop shipping answers both these questions. A business can be run without having a physical location or an office. Drop shipping doesn't require a retailer to have inventory or a warehouse to store their product.

Drop shipping is an option for businesses that do not stock the goods. The retailer receives an order form a customer. They then transfer the order to the product manufacture, another retailer, or wholesaler. Finally, the customer is shipped the product. The retailer acts as an intermediary between the customer's manufacturer and wholesaler. The retailer does not have to ship or package the goods like the manufacturer or wholesaler.

The difference between wholesalers' prices and customer prices is what the retailer makes a profit. Sometimes, however the manufacturer or wholesaler may pay some commission to the retailer for the sale.

This business is extremely admirable, as the retailer needs only a laptop or desktop computer and an internet connection.

It's important to know that drop shipping is also used by businesses with physical addresses. This saves time and helps to free up space.

As the terms can sometimes be interchangeable in the business world, there is confusion about who is a wholesaler, drop ship manufacturer or aggregator. This is how it works: the dropship producer is the one that makes the commodity in question. The wholesaler orders products in bulk from the manufacturer. They then package them and sell the products to customers via online retailers. The retailer can choose from a range of products offered by the aggregator by purchasing different products at different dropship wholesalers. This saves the retailer time and money by not having to place separate orders with different wholesalers.

Sometimes, retailers may have a physical shop where customers can inspect the products. You can also see the products online. To keep the wholesale origin of the product secret, they use blind shipping.

Drop shipping is common for expensive products. This is particularly true if the retailer receives large orders. The manufacturer can arrange to ship the goods directly from the retailer.

Drop shipping can be a great idea for someone starting out in online business. Drop shipping is low-risk, and only requires a small capital investment. It is ideal for store owners who have a business and want to try new products.

Drop shipping is an ideal venture for the following entrepreneurs.

An online business requires traffic to be successful. It can take time to build that traffic and turn it into cash. Drop shipping requires little capital to begin. You will need more marketing skills than you have financial ability to make drop shipping a viable business model. It's ideal for first-timers who are just getting started with passive income. This allows them the opportunity to start an online business and learn how to drive traffic.

Drop shipping is also an option for Walmart entrepreneurs who deal with many different products. It can be hard to trade in large quantities and different products if finances are tight. Drop shipping works well as a business model, as you don't have to have the funds. You get the order from the wholesaler and have it shipped to the customer.

Drop shipping is an option for budget entrepreneurs. Drop shipping is an affordable option, as you don't need stock to start with. Drop shipping can be a viable option for people who don't have enough funds or want to keep the transaction budget low.

Drop shipping is an ideal business model for entrepreneurs who require product validation before investing. Drop shipping can be used for testing new products in the marketplace and evaluating their performance before you decide to invest.

Dropshipping should not be practiced by anyone

Drop shipping is not an option for entrepreneurs who wish to preserve a brand. It's not easy to build a brand, let alone push it to new heights. Most importantly, you need to have control over your customer so you can choose what they get. Drop shipping is a way to limit your control over the customer. Sometimes, a wholesaler or manufacturer may send a product to your customer in an unsatisfying packaging. However, you do not have control over the shipping. Drop shipping is a risky option for customers who are looking to build a reputation and keep it going.

Drop shipping can be a lucrative option if you have a high profit margin in mind. Drop shipping can present a challenge due to its low profit margins. After you subtract the amount you charge wholesaler for the product, the profit margin drops to between 10-20%. Once you subtract the cost of credit card debits and email costs, the margin is even lower. This strategy will only work if there is a steady high level of sales.

Drop shipping does not work for retailers who lack creativity. Let's face facts: Many wholesalers and manufacturers now sell their products through ecommerce sites. You will then be competing with your supplier if you wish to sell their products. The retailer will get a much larger profit margin than you, which can be a problem. This means that you must be more creative in order to make money selling their products. You need to find gaps in their sales cycle and fill them. This means that Facebook ads are not enough.

How do you determine which products are best to sell?

Drop shipping is a key factor in your success. What criteria do you use when deciding on the right product to sell?

The following are some factors to consider:

The retail price. As we know, the retailer maximizes the difference between selling the product and paying the drop shipper. Pricing your product can be very important. While a product priced low may be attractive to potential buyers, the final result will be low returns.

The product's longevity. There is a possibility of repeat orders if the product that you sell can be reused or thrown away. This will increase the sales of your product and extend your income.

The product's turn-over rate is important. Retailers should look for products that are stable over time. This is because the quality of your product photography and the information you have posted about it are crucial. If you are looking for products that can change, you will need to continue updating the information. This is both time-consuming as well as costly.

Consider cross-selling. A great idea is to sell products that can be used together. Selling suits with matching shoes is a great idea. Your customer will then be more likely to buy both the suits and the shoes together. This is possible by pricing the main product lower and selling it together with the other products.

The product's dimensions and weight. Drop shipping a product is expensive depending on its size and weight. Smaller and lighter products will cost you less to ship than heavier ones. You'll also make the most of your profits. For beginners, it's better to start with small products.

How to Develop an Online Drop Shipping Business

Drop shipping can be easy, as it requires less capital and more marketing skills. But, you will need to spend a lot of time researching before you can actually start. You can use the following steps to start or develop a drop-shipping business.

Niche selection. Picking the right niche is important. If you pick a niche that is not relevant to your interests, it may be difficult to market it effectively. This could be discouraging, as marketing is an important part of any business. It is important to choose a niche that will generate profits and attract impulse buyers. It should also ship cheaply. It should also be easy to ship.

You should conduct competition research. It is crucial to remember that drop shipping companies will face established businesses. It is important to do your research on the products you will be working with. It is common to choose products with lower competition. Products with no completion do not have any demand. This could be due to low profit margins, high shipping costs or manufacturing problems. Products with high competition are therefore more in demand.

Find a supplier. After conducting competition research, you can then search for a reliable supplier. It can be disastrous for your company if you choose the wrong supplier. Your business is now online so you need to be extra careful when choosing your supplier. You should do your due diligence before you choose a supplier. Communication with the supplier is essential to avoid any problems like late shipping or poor packaging that could cause customer dissatisfaction. Ask as many questions as you can about the supplier, and you will get the answers you need. Know their production capabilities. It is possible to seek guidance from other drop shippers in order to get some best practices.

You can start an ecommerce website. For this to happen, you need to be able to use technology. It's not necessary to start huge. You don't have to start large. Once your business has established itself, you can then start thinking about customizing your website to suit your needs.

Plan how you will acquire customers. Everyone can agree that no matter how well-respected your business is, whether you have the best website, the best niche or the best connection to the best supplier, none of that will be helpful without customers. Your business' success is dependent on the customers who purchase from you. Your sales strategy should focus on attracting clients and making them return customers. Facebook ads can be a very useful tool. Target customers that might be interested and create targeted ads. Long-term search engine optimization is something you should consider as your business grows. You should also look into email marketing to expand your customer base.

Analyze the progress of your business and make improvements. Your business will improve and you will need an analysis of your progress. Keep track of who you have attracted customers to you and when they purchased. You should look at the things that have worked for you, and then try to improve them. Also, take a look at what didn't go well and work to change it. For increased sales, you can think of new marketing and promotion strategies.

Is Drop Shipping Legal?

Drop shipping as a method of managing supply chains is legal. What you do in business is quite another. If the customer receives a product that is not up to standard, they might choose to shop with you. This is when the illegalities begin to appear. Additionally, illegalities can sneak in if copyrights are infringed.

Drop shipping offers many benefits

Drop shipping businesses are easy to start. You don't need a large amount of financial capital. All you need to start is a computer connected to the internet. Once you have identified a supplier, you will receive orders. You can then make your money. It's easy for beginners to grasp.

There are no additional costs that the investor must incur when setting up a new business. These can include renting, buying, or renting an office or warehouse, paying electricity bills and so forth.

The website charges are the only charge that the business owner will have to pay.

Drop shipping business has minimal risk. Even if the products do not sell, the retailer isn't at risk as nothing expires. The investor isn't under any pressure to dispose of the stock.

There are many products that retailers can deal in. After the investor has chosen their niche, there will be a variety of products and suppliers who can ship those products. The investor has the option of focusing on one product or a combination of products.

In order to increase profits in ordinary businesses, you must invest more capital and work harder. Drop shipping is a business model that allows the entrepreneur to send more orders. This will increase the profits. The wholesaler then takes care of the rest while you take advantage of the profits.

Drop Shipping's Disadvantages

Drop shipping can bring in a small profit margin. The difference between what the customer pays and what the retailer sells to them is called the retailer's profit. Other fees, including credit card costs, can reduce the retailer's profit and make it smaller.

Even if the supplier was at fault, any problem that occurs is still the responsibility of the retailer. If the supplier makes a mistake, the retailer is still liable. When choosing a supplier, the retailer should be careful.

Drop shipping is very cost-effective. Drop shipping has seen a rise in popularity and more people are now aware of it. If the retailer fails to think of a niche, they may lose business to the competition.

It can be hard to keep track and monitor the stock levels of suppliers. A retailer might be responsible for cancelling orders or placing backorders if they don't communicate well.

Chapter 6: 11 Proven Investment Strategies That Work For A Small Amount Of Money

It may seem like a ridiculous amount to invest, but it is actually a sufficient amount to get started with an investment that will generate income. It could also help you become a skilled investor who owns many successful businesses if you continue to invest the returns.

When we read or hear about the successes stories of wealthy businessmen who built large fortunes by investing amounts not equal to a weekly cup coffee, we ask ourselves if that is possible.

Here are 11 proven ways you can successfully invest a small amount.

Forex

YouTube videos can be used to help you learn Forex. After this, you can create a free demo account. Demo accounts allow you to trade with fake money. You can then open a real account to trade real money once you've completed the training.

It is possible to gain many benefits from your past experience if you learn well and were able to take risks. You must demonstrate calm, rationality, ability to take risks, lack in recklessness, speed, understanding, intuition and fast internet.

Electronic project

Start an online business for less than $100 Start a blog, which you can do for as low $20, or create an online shop using platforms like Shopify and Amazon to sell your products or services. You can also purchase a microphone to use with your smartphone and wallpaper to create videos for YouTube.

Shops in the Home

Anyone can buy an apartment, or any one of the rooms within it, and turn it into their own store. This will allow them to make sales and earn money. For example you can create 10 tops with $ 100 and have them available for sale in your apartment. Your neighbors and residents can help you promote your products and make it easy for them to purchase the product.

The products you offer will be a hit and you'll quickly make a profit. You can use these profits for reinvestment in your company to buy more clothes and better equip your place for the growth of your business. This example can be extended to beauty products, home food, etc. - have fun!

Dealing in secondhand goods

You can buy large quantities, including valuable pens and glasses, and then resell them at an increased price to your neighbors, acquaintances, online, or as part of exhibitions.

Petroleum oil

For $30, you could buy a set if used jerrycans (10 liters) and use them to collect oil from the small restaurants in your neighborhood at low prices. Then, sell them to soap manufacturers at a price that makes you a good profit.

It is notable that this work has grown in popularity, and many restaurants now deal directly or indirectly with soap factories. Many small restaurants are not aware of this and do not deal with soap factories. This is a chance to buy at the lowest price, and then resell to factories that offer the highest profit.

Products for the domestic market

You can make many different products such as soap, shampoo and other recipes. You can make household products at home by purchasing the required materials. These types projects can be started for less than $100, but it takes patience and determination to succeed.

7. Home farming

If you have a large balcony, or you have the space to plant plants on the roof of the home or building you live in, then you may be able to buy a bunch of plant pots. A group of vegetable seed can be purchased and planted in these pots. They will grow until you sell them or you enjoy them. This is an excellent indirect way to invest in your home.

Vegetable trade

For a small investment, you can purchase a set of vegetable boxes that are highly in demand at the wholesale marketplace and resell them at retail for profit. This is a simple business venture that allows you to reinvest the money to buy more vegetables. You will also be able to increase your profit if you continue to resell and buy more. So, for example, if your net profit was $ 25 and you purchased $ 100 worth of vegetables, you can buy more vegetables next year for $ 12.

Invest in your self

For high-income skills, you can take an online class or participate in a live training program. A skill with a high income is one that can make you more than $10,000. It's a skill you can apply anywhere.

Investment in yourself can result in "selling the skill": programming, copywriting web design, online marketing coaching, teaching and entrepreneurship.

10. Your car can turn into a project

You do not need a taxi license to transform your car into one. Uber is open to anyone who has a car and a valid license. The operating system is a set of rules that Uber shares with its drivers. You do not need to commit to a particular time.

Any of the above ideas can be implemented immediately if you are interested. These ideas do not require a lot of investment. Also, the chance of failure is very slim. This gives you the possibility to grow the business into something bigger.

If these ideas don't convince you, then you can sit quietly with yourself and contemplate how to invest $100.

Sure, there will be many ideas. However, choose the most relevant one and begin to implement it now.

Chapter 7: Choosing Stocks To Invest In

After researching the stock markets and the opportunities it offers, it's important to take the time to select the right stocks. There are many stocks on the market. But not all of them can provide you with a good return. Some of these companies will give you the best chances to make money while minimizing the risk. Others will fail right away. You might be worried about how to choose the best stocks for you.

First, you must remember that you cannot just buy a stock because someone told you it was good. You should do your own research. It is possible to listen to the advice of friends and brokers, but this is your money and you should be the one who controls it. Do your research and you'll quickly discover the best stocks for you regardless of what anyone else says.

If you have already done your research and have a list that you like, go to their website.

You can find information on their stocks on almost all of them. This will help you make a decision. Look at all their financial reports, as this will show you the company's market performance. You'll be amazed at how much information is available about a company simply by looking around.

There are many things to take into consideration when picking a stock, but you must choose one that is going to make you money. You should avoid picking stocks that you know will be expensive or that you cannot earn. Only choose winners. Here are some tips to help you limit your risks:

The company's margin for profit.

A company's total debts, and the amount of those debts.

Return on equity in that company.

The ratio of equity and debt. This is a useful indicator that will help you determine how your company spends their money, and whether they do it responsibly.

It is important to know how the company has performed in the past. Also, whether the company is expected to do it again, better or worse.

What should you be looking for?

Perhaps you're curious about the things to look out for when selecting a company to invest. Charts and graphs are a great way to check out how a stock has performed in the stock market. However, this is just one part of the story. Also, it is worth looking at the company in order to assess its ability to sustain that status long-term. One example is that a company may look great on the charts and graphs. But if they don't have the ability to save money or manage their debts well, it might not be right for you. You should look at the following things when choosing a stock:

Who manages the business

This is the first thing to do when investing in a company. This will give you an insight into the current and future performance of the company. Many newcomers consider management of a business not that important. But, even a well-run company can sink quickly if the management is not competent.

Before you decide to invest, you should carefully examine the management of the company. A few factors to consider include the return of equity, which is the percentage of shareholders still earning profit each year. If the equity return for the company is higher than five percent, it is likely that the company will continue to grow and do well. Look at the relationships between the management and their employees. Are they getting along well and making the right decisions for the company?

Pick a sector which is doing well

It is important to choose stocks from businesses that are also performing well when picking stocks. Depending on the state of the economy, some industries might still be able to thrive in a downturn. Others may fare better. There will be times when the economy does well, but only a few industries are doing as well.

This is why it's so important to focus your efforts on industries that are doing well. Also, you might want to spread your money so that you are not in financial trouble if one industry fails. You should only choose industries that are expected to prosper over a long period. If you feel that an industry isn't performing well, it's easy to sell it and find another.

Profits increasing

A company that makes profits is another important consideration. You won't get a return on your investment if you see a business that is losing money. You want to ensure that the company has increased profits each year. If the company continues to grow its profits, it is doing well. This is a sign that they are popular and growing in popularity. This makes it a popular investment option. The greater your profits are, the higher your return on investment.

The size and scope of your company

Some investors would prefer to work for a smaller company. They believe these companies will be easier to work alongside and they will be better able to monitor than bigger companies. Some studies have shown that smaller companies actually face more risks than larger companies.

This is because many larger companies have taken their time in getting established. They weren't established overnight, so they can be considered safe investments. It is often better to invest in a bigger company than you have experience with the stock market. You can choose to work with a smaller business if you feel confident about your knowledge of the stock exchange and the risks you are willing to take.

A beginner should avoid penny stocks. These are sometimes tempting because they can be so cheap to work with. These companies are extremely risky. Often, they don't have to disclose financial information to investors and users. If you decide to invest in penny stocks, it is possible that you could lose a lot. It is better to stick with the top companies on stock market to ensure that you have more options.

Look at the dividends

If a company looks good, make sure you check if they have the ability to pay dividends. It is great to begin your career with companies that can share their profits. This means that the company is capable of managing their debts and sharing the profits with shareholders. It is possible that they will do it again, and you will continue to get these payments in future.

If you're deciding on how much you can earn with dividend payments, make sure you choose a company capable of paying you at least two per cent. This is a good indicator that the company is steady and that you can expect to be able make a good amount of money each fiscal year. Finding one with a higher profit margin than the 2 percent is a good sign.

Manageable debt

As you consider which companies to invest in you should also take a look into their debts. You don't have the company to be debt-free. However, you should ensure that there is a healthy balance between the amount that they take on as well as the amount that they are able make.

A company can have good debts especially if it's just started or recently expanded. You might have some debts to pay for your buildings, your equipment, or other items. Although it's unlikely to find a company without debt, you should still look for one with a manageable debt load for the profits they make each fiscal year. If they have so many debts that they are unable to cover them each month, you should look elsewhere. You will lose money if they can't manage that debt.

You should choose liquid stocks

You should also consider how liquid the stocks you are considering investing in. Liquid stocks are best because they are easy to sell and buy. Stocks that are not liquid may make it difficult to sell the stock when you decide to exit the market. Most stocks will have some form of liquidity. But the more liquid the stock, the easier it can be for you to trade it when you wish.

Look for a stock that offers a happy medium. You want it to be a reasonable price. However, you don't want to see too much demand. If the demand for it is too high, it may be too costly to get it. The demand must be sufficiently high that someone is willing to buy stocks from you when it is time to exit the market.

When it comes to choosing the right stocks, there are many factors you should consider. When you are looking for stocks to sell, do your research. You will need to find out who the company is managed by, what their profit and their debts are, and which stocks they have. This will ensure that you find secure and good stocks that will allow you to make a decent profit.

Chapter 8: Risk Tolerance

It is vital that you decide your personal risk tolerance when you start investing. You also need to consider whether or not you are comfortable with being exposed to the stock, bond, and real estate markets. There are no guarantees in investing in the stock, bond or real estate markets. There are many questionnaires that you can use online to determine how comfortable your money is being invested. For a more accurate assessment of your risk tolerance, I recommend that you consult with your financial advisor.

Financial advisors will use your age as a metric to evaluate how long you are likely to live until you die. The lower your risk, the more you can afford to lose your money. Talking about the following points with your financial advisor (or representatives from 401(k), will help you to determine how much risk you are able to take.

Are there any major expenses you are planning to make, like buying a home or paying college fees?

Do your current financial earnings (cash flow), cover your living expenses

Are you paying ongoing medical expenses?

Are you deeply in credit card and other debts?

Are you sure that you have sufficient health insurance?

Are you financially prepared in the event of your unemployment?

It is vital to share a complete picture with your financial advisor (or 401(k), representatives) to help them determine the appropriate risk. Talk to your financial adviser about the following bullet points. You should never hide information from your financial adviser. You can think of it as going to the doctor and not sharing all of your symptoms.

Without all of your symptoms, how will the doctor be able provide the best diagnosis?

To help you assess your risk tolerance, consider how comfortable it will be to accept a correction of 15% to 20% in the market. You will lose sleep at night worrying about how your account is doing. Markets can go up or down. It is crucial that you feel comfortable with your portfolio and are confident in your ability to manage risk.

What is a Mutual Fund, and what are its benefits?

What is a "mutual fund"? The simple answer to this question is: A mutual trust is a shopping list of stocks and/or securities that is managed individually by money managers. These individuals buy and sell stock/bonds within mutual funds. By purchasing shares in mutual funds, you basically buy small parts of stocks and/or bonds. This allows for diversification and reduces stock-specific risk.

Let's look closer at Vanguard Equity Income Fund, one mutual fund. Go to Vanguard's website. Select the Vanguard Equity Income Fund. The mutual fund symbol for VEIPX is displayed on the first page. It will then include the overview of the mutual fund. This overview is crucial as it contains information such as the mutual fund's product summary and asset class, category. Portfolio composition, price, and more. Let's dive into some of these points.

Let's get started with the Product summary. This summary will explain the mutual fund's investment strategy, and its objective. The Vanguard Equity Income's investment objective makes it clear that the money manager wants to invest only in stocks that consistently pay dividends and not in fast-growing businesses.

Let's take a closer look at that. Stocks are usually classified as either a Growth Stock, or a Value Stock. Growth stocks are companies that are young and new, or are experiencing rapid growth in their industry. Amazon is a great example of growth stock. A Value Stock is a stock that is older and has experienced small to moderate growth. Verizon is a good example for a value stock. A value stock pays a dividend to shareholders more often that not.

A dividend is an amount paid by a corporation to its shareholders. Dividends, unlike bank rates, are not guaranteed. When a company is in trouble, and they need to keep as many cash as possible within the corporation, they might reduce or eliminate paying dividends. In other words, Verizon, a mutual fund called Vanguard Equity Income Fund is one of their stocks that they hold as long as it meets their investment strategy.

Next you will want to check the Mutual Fund's Asset class. The asset class indicates where the money manger is buying and/or selling bonds and stocks for the fund. Are money managers buying a mixture stock and bond? Are they buying stocks/bonds in the United

States and/or internationally? Vanguard Equity Income Fund is a money manager that trades stocks within the United States. This asset class is called Domestic Stock General. As we go along, you'll see that this information is crucial when determining how your investments should be asset-allocated.

The category summary will generally mirror that of the mutual fund. One important point about the category will be that it will indicate whether the fund is investing or not in large-cap, mid-cap, or small-cap companies. These terms will be discussed in a future chapter. If you examine the Vanguard Equity Income Fund category, you will see that it is labeled Large Value. This means they invest only in Large Cap Value stocks.

Portfolio Composition is something you may be less interested in. But it is useful to understand how the money manager splits the money between the stocks that they are buying. Vanguard Equity Income Fund appears to hold stocks in several industries including Financials and Health Care. You will see JPMorgan Chase & Co. is the largest holding (Financial Industry), followed closely by Johnson & Johnson for Health Care Industry. Let's examine the top 10 holdings in the fund at the time of writing.

Industries of companies

JPMorgan Chase & Co. Financial

Johnson & Johnson Health Care

Verizon Communications, Inc. Communication Services

Cisco Systems Inc. Information Technology

Pfizer Inc. Health Care

Chevron Corp. Energy

Merck & Company Inc. Health Care

Communication Services at Comcast Corp.

Intel Corp. Information Technology

Bank of America Corp.

If you look at the overall Portfolio Composition for the mutual fund, you'll see that the money manager has spread their investments across many categories.

Industry Mutual Funds Investment Percentage

Communications Services 7.10%

Consumer discretionary 4.10%

Consumer Staples 12.79%

Energy 8.80%

Financials 17.20%

Health Care 17.00%

Industrials 9.80%

Information Technology 10.40%

Materials 3.20%

Real Estate 1.40%

8.30% on Utilities

Knowing which categories your mutual fund invests in can help you make a decision about whether or not you want to join that fund. If the outlook for the energy sector is dire and you have concerns about how the economy will perform in the future, your representative can advise you on whether investing in a fund that holds a high proportion of energy stocks.

Lastly, you'll see how much the mutual fund costs per share. This is known as the mutual funds' NAV (net asset valuation). As with buying stock, the mutual funds' NAV is the cost per share. A mutual fund with a NAV $10 would allow you to buy 1,000 shares. The NAV of a mutual funds fluctuates every day depending on the performance of stocks or bonds within it. Vanguard says that the NAV calculation is done by adding all assets to a fund and subtracting liabilities. The result is then divided by the total shares outstanding.

You will also see the overview page's expense ratio, minimum required investment, yield, total number stocks, and other details. The expense ratio represents how much money you are paying to the money manager for the fund's management. The minimum amount you have to invest to purchase the mutual fund is called the minimum investment. The dividend payment you receive is known as the yield. The total number or stocks in the mutual fund will show you how well-diversified it is. NAV pricing can fluctuate more in mutual funds that have 50 stocks, compared to mutual funds that have 300 stocks.

Chapter 9: Habits Of Investment - The Beginner's Stage

We enjoy hearing stories about people who have achieved fame in their field of business or entertainment. We want to feel that person's success. The idea of being successful is not something to be ashamed of. People don't fail because they lack funds, but because of how they approach investing.

Now that we have an overview of the common terms in the financial market, and that we know some strategies that will help us achieve our investment goals, let's start building our investment habits.

Start Today

The biggest misconception about investing is that you should start earlier than you are today. It is easy to say "I want" and then go on to say "I will invest!" The thought of "I want it to be an investment" is often followed by "I would only do it when my capital is sufficient". We didn't save enough for the future. Then we realized that we should not have. Successive investors believe that the earlier you start, your chances of achieving great returns are higher. Even if your budget is not large enough to invest in the big-time markets, it's possible to start investing even a modest sum. There are plenty of investment opportunities that offer you the chance to invest and get the future returns.

It is vital to understand that you should make investing a top priority now and not regret later. This will be the first step in your investment success.

It is important to research the cost and make an informed decision.

A successful investor is not just a risk-taker; they are also wise. Many successful investors would tell you, if you look at articles about them, that they had researched and studied the topic before they invested. If not managed well, investment can lead to catastrophic results. While it is a good way to grow your assets and may be a good way to make money, it can also bring you great opportunities to build wealth. It is important to research the investment cost before you invest. The best way to decide if you are making the right investment is to research it. Remember to always strive for the best in investing. Some people think that looking at assets cost is a waste and not helpful. While this might be true at times, it is most often false. It is best to do your research to learn more about the assets that interest you in order to avoid falling into the traps of financial market.

Stock market fluctuation is a common phenomenon. It means that prices can change without any pattern. If the product you purchased didn't live up to your expectations, it would be a disappointment. This is why you need to make a habit of doing a lot of research. It has been said many times that an investment is like a game. Chess players do more than move their pieces randomly to complete the game. They also move it strategically to defend their king. Think of your king as your assets and your opponent as the financial market. You have to win the game while protecting the King in order to control the market. This requires a lot of thought before you can move. This is because chess can take a lot of time. It is also a chance to exercise patience. If you aren't doing your research and knowing the costs, you can be impatient about the results of your investment. The process of waiting is key to achieving a higher rate return.

A second thing you need to know is the terms of investment deals. Most people click the checkbox to confirm that they have read and understood the terms and conditions.

Be sure to take the time necessary to thoroughly read any deal, regardless of whether it's about the stock markets or business opportunities. Be aware that this is about the investment risks. You're not playing with your queen. Without understanding the game, it's almost like playing chess sans any strategy.

Research is not enough to give you enough information on an investment. However, it can help you be consistent with your decisions. It will help you allocate your assets in the most profitable investment opportunities by keeping track of the costs. This habit can help you have better future returns.

Passive Investments: Which one should you choose?

Other than the strategies discussed at the beginning, the third habit you should establish is the practice of choosing passive investments during the early stages of your investment. Passive Investment means minimizing your investment buying/selling and maximising your long-term return. This strategy is well-tested and has proven to be a successful one.

Many people believed that investing in the future meant taking risks. Although this is true, it's important to keep your risk-taking down in the initial stages. This is how you build your empire. An empire can't be built in one day. It takes time to build, but it will last a lifetime. These structures, along with many others around the globe, are still highly valued and very motivating. Investors should avoid investing too much to get higher future returns. This strategy allows you to gradually build your wealth up until it blossoms.

Another benefit to passive investment is that there are no hidden fees. This will enable you to save money for future investment. Passive investment allows beginners to avoid spending their time researching and analyzing financial statements. Investors love this strategy, even though it is familiar to them. It offers high returns and minimal risk.

You must have a diverse portfolio in order to make this habit work. It is important to not put all your eggs within one basket. You should also spread them across multiple baskets. The following are other benefits of this habit:

Passive Investment comes with low fees. Each investor strives to minimize investment costs and maximize their profit. This is why passive investing is so appealing to people. This investment option has low fees, which can help to reduce the risk of hidden charges. Taxes are also easier to pay. This strategy lowers capital gain taxes, which is great for investors.

Transparency. Investors do not have to spend too much time researching the company's financial performance. Instead, they would just look at the index fund and consider which assets have a lower expense.

Simple. This strategy is more easily understood than the complexity of understanding investment dynamics. Despite our eagerness for everything, it is not easy to understand. It is difficult to comprehend the financial market for those who are just starting in the business. Passive investment is the best method to invest without taking too much risk.

There are many advantages to passive investment but also some downsides when it comes time to use it as long-term investment. These are:

Limitation. Passive investing has many limitations. The pre-determined list of investments that investors can choose from has very little variability. This limit the investor's options for expanding their market position.

You can expect small returns. You can expect low-risk investment to yield returns, but that doesn't mean you should expect too much. Passive investment is a slow way to beat the market, but it will never provide high returns for investors unless the markets tell you otherwise. This is why most investors only use passive investing for a brief time to help them build their investment foundation and then look for another strategy.

The first three habits mentioned aim to strengthen your foundation when it is time to develop the right investor mindset. As you gain confidence in your decision making skills, you'll be able use these habits to help you see the bigger picture and plan for what you can do next to become an effective investor.

Chapter 10: Swing-Trading Stocks

Here are some of these differences between Swing Trading and Day Trading. Day Trading is also known as 'Day Trading' because it involves a certain period of time. Swing Trading stock also has a specific span of time. Swing Trading's time span is longer than day-trading, but shorter than someone who is 'investing or in for long term. A trading period of less than one year is considered short-term for tax and accounting reasons. Anything longer than a year will be considered 'long term'.

Swing trading can be described as a different style of trading. Swing trading is for individuals who would prefer to be involved in trades longer than day traders. Day traders will rarely let a trade remain in effect overnight. They will often enter and exit the same trade on the same day. Swing traders will keep their trade open for several weeks, or even months.

Pros and Con of Swing Trading Stocks

Swing Trading Stocks is like everything else. There are good sides and bad sides to swing trading stocks.

Swing traders of stocks believe they are less at risk than day traders. Although they may be able to comprehend their thinking processes, it is likely that they are both equally dangerous depending on how experienced, psychological, and technical analysis techniques are used by trader. While everyone believes that long-term investment is safer than short term, the latest statistics prove that this is not always the case. According to me, the more a trade is exposed the markets, then the greater risk it carries. Many people believe that investing is too complicated and should not be done by anyone. Instead, they should trust the brokerage to keep their money safe.

The Pros and Cons of Swing Trading Stocks

Day trading takes less time than day trading. Traders have more time between trades for analysis, which could lead to better traders.

A trader can take the time to correct a poor entry and then return to a positive situation depending on which direction he has chosen. This will usually be better than an initial short position.

Swing Traders don't have to meet the 'Pattern Day Trader' requirements.

Swing traders can access more data (timeframe wise) than day trader. Swing traders are more confident in their trades due to the fact that they have access to longer-term historical data.

The Cons of Swing Trading Stocks (double sided swords from Pros mentioned above)

Day trading takes less time than day trading. Traders have more time to conduct analysis between trades, which could lead to better traders.

Con: Swing traders may also include bad information in their data analysis to choose stocks that are less profitable or losing.

A trader can take the time to correct a poor entry and then return to a positive situation depending on the direction he has chosen. This will usually be better than an initial short position.

Con: Your trade can be affected by a poor entry.

Any trader whether swing trader or day trader needs to be fully aware of their trades and the risks involved. Here's a short checklist of things you should look for before entering into trades.

The following questions will help you assess your confidence:

Psychology of the Trade

Are you in control your Greeds, Fears, Patience, and Desperation? Otherwise, you might make a hasty trade. Make sure that you are only trading disposable capital to avoid any impulsive decisions.

Up (Long), or Down (Short).

The most fundamental question before entering a trade is the one that every trade will answer. Is the stock going up or down? How did you arrive at this conclusion? Do you have evidence from outside sources to support your answer? If you can't support your answer with evidence from outside sources, then it might not be true and you may consider not entering the market at all.

Trust in your strategy

Are you able to prove your technical indicators? These indicators have you ever used in paper trading, or with other trades? They have worked well for you. Simple Moving Averages (or Exponential moving averages) tend to be the most consistent technical indicators.

DAY TRADING & SWING TRADING

Swing trading is similar to day trading. Both trading styles aim to make money on short movements in the market. They are not for everyone. The risk is offset by the potential for great returns. Nothing compares to the thrill of completing an extremely successful trade. Some trades last only minutes while others may take days.

Swing trades and Day Trading are two different things. Swing trades are more rigid. Day traders tend to be out at the close of each day and often do multiple trades daily. This allows you to see where you are at the close each day. Swing trades are not guaranteed to close within a single day. They are however more likely to continue for several days. Also, the trades are more likely than others to end in a short time. While swing trading has the potential to make more, there are also some risks. Swing trading or day trading may be your ticket to quitting your day job if it is possible.

Day trading doesn't have overnight risks provided that all trades are done before the market closes. Swing trades have a greater vulnerability to the economic and news climate during the trading days or at night. You can be affected by news that is outside the control of your swing trade system. Without a system, swing trading or day trading will likely not be profitable.

Day trading and swing trading systems start at $2000. From there, it can increase. You can find a wide variety of approaches that traders use to build a winning strategy. While there are many approaches you can take to building your trading system, the key is to keep it consistent. No matter what the market direction, there are always great opportunities in day trading or swing trades in all markets.

As long as you follow your rules for trading signals, it is possible to trade multiple stocks on a daily basis. Trades with the same stock portfolio can help you get a sense of what stocks will do in the event of economic changes or news. A reliable stock picking resource can help you filter out bad stocks and identify new stocks.

It is important to set up a system that covers both swing trades parameters as well new stock picks. This keeps you away from emotions and the day trading process. A stock that is successful in day trading may not perform well in swing trading.

Comparing Swing Trading and Day Trading

Day trading involves opening and closing trades on the same day. Day trading is dominated by the phenomenon of resistance and support. Day trading activities depend on the existence of daily trends. Day trading relies on buyers and sellers' fizzling emotions. The interaction between bubble emotions, i.e., greed and fear, is called day trading. Investors' mindset (i.e. bear, bull, etc.) can lead to capital gain or loss.

Normally, the price of shares moves in a pattern with frequent swings. This phenomenon is called swings and it offers capital gain opportunities. Swing trading refers to an investment activity that involves holding a tradable commodity for a period of one to several days, in order to gain from price fluctuations or'swings. Swing traders are not able to place trades daily. Swing trading can offer a larger profit potential that day trading. Swing trading requires patience and a better understanding of the stock market. Investors may trade for days or even weeks. It all depends on how well stock trends/swings perform. Swing traders have a general satisfaction level about the length of their swings. However, unexpected trends or shorter swings can cause anxiety and disrupt the comfort zone. This is why novice swing investors might not be able to take quick decisions. Swing trading requires calm behavior and thorough technical research of the share, industry, and economy. Swing trading is a skill that allows you to buy when people have sold and sell when there are buyers. This is done by having a greater understanding of the future trends and swings. He enjoys riding the trend until it reverses or retraces. Swing-traders can be told by market experts that "retracements" are price reversals of temporary nature that occur within a larger trend. The important thing is that price reversals in this context are only temporary and do not signal a change of the larger trend. Trends that do not retrace are unhealthy and dangerous. Because a trend can be defined as "a series of higher lows and higher highs", then the trend must cease when the stock fails or sets a lower high. It is possible for a stock to set a lower high, but this does not mean that it has ended the trend. It is possible for a stock to retrace once it has established a lower high. However, the stock will not set a lower lowest low and could then move above the previous high in search of a higher high. The setting of a lower high is the key to a bullish tendency. Trends are usually over once the lower low is established. This is known as a Reversal.

Day trading can be profitable if the investor sets small goals. Swing trading offers investors much more lucrative targets. A better understanding of market trends, and the behavioral strength of investors towards these trends is key to achieving targets. While a non-strategist or impatient loses money, a strategist and patient make more. If day trading targets seem feasible but swing trading targets seem uncertain, this is a tradeoff. A tradeoff is when one target can be achieved at the expense the other. In other words, swing trading profit is day trading profit and swing trading profit is day trading profit. Swing traders are more inclined to earn dividends and therefore act proactive during book closure days.

PROBLEMS WITH SWING TRADING

USEING OPTIONS

Swing trading can be one of most popular methods to trade the stock market. Swing trading has been around for many years. Swing trading refers to buying now and then selling days, weeks, or even months later when prices have dropped or gone up (in the instance of a short). These price swings are also known as "Price Swings", hence the term "Swing Trading".

Options trading is used by most options traders as leverage. They may want to buy call option when they are cheap and then quickly sell them for a leveraged advantage. This is also true for put option. But, these novice traders quickly discovered the hard way that options swing trading can result in significant losses, even if the stock does move in the direction they expected.

How is this possible? What are the potential problems of swing trading with options that they have not considered?

Even though options can be used simply as leveraged replacement for trading the underlying stocks, there are still some important things that novice traders fail to remember.

Strike price

It doesn't take much for anyone to realize there are many options, at many strike prices, for all optionsable stocks. A common choice for beginners is to choose the "cheapest" option that offers higher leverage. Options with no built-in value can be taken out of money options. These are either call options that have strike values higher than current stock prices or put options that have strike rates lower than current stock prices.

You have to be careful when buying out-of-the-money options in swing trade. The stock could move in your direction for buying call options or downwards for purchasing put options. However, you can still lose ALL of your money if it does not exceed your option strike price. This is what's known as "Expire out Of The Money", and it renders all the options useless. This is also why most options trading novices lose all of their money.

The more money options have, the greater the leverage. Also, there is a higher chance that they will lose their value and all of your money. The higher the option's value, the less leverage they offer and the lower their risk of being worthless. When swing trading with options with strike prices, you need to think about the potential magnitude of the move. A big move is possible with the out of money options. However, if it fails to exceed the expiration strike price, you may be in for a rude awakening.

Expiration date

Swing trading with stocks is a way to hold on to your stock portfolio forever, but options have a fixed expiration date. This means that, if you are not right, you will quickly lose money.

Swing trading using options is like fighting against time. The greater the stock's movement, the more you can expect to profit. There are options for all optionable stocks that can be traded across many expiration month periods. This is a good thing. The options that fall within the first month of an option are usually cheaper than those that fall within the second month. However, they are generally more expensive. If you are certain that the underlying stock will move quickly you might trade with options closer to expiration, otherwise known as "Front Month Opportunities", which are typically cheaper and have a higher leverage. You could opt for a second expiration date, which is more costly and will allow the stock to move more slowly.

Therefore, swing trading with options requires you to choose between leverage or time. Profitable options can be sold even before expiration dates. Swing traders typically choose options that have 2 to 3 more months before they expire.

Extrinsic Value

Extrinsic or "premium" is the part of an option's cost that expires with no refund. Because of this, all the money options listed above become worthless upon expiration. Because the entire price of these money options consists only in Extrinsic Valuation and no builtin value (intrinsic).

Extrinsic values are subject to erosion under two conditions. Time decay, or the erosion of extrinsic worth over time as expiration approaches, can be described as "Time Decay". Option that are not profitable become less valuable over time and may eventually cease to be worth any value. Swing trading with options involves a race against time. The higher your probability of making a profit, the faster the stock moves. This is in contrast to swing trading with the stock, which allows you to make a profit for as long as the stock moves eventually.

The "Volatility Crunch" refers to the erosion of intrinsic value caused by stock market "excitement", or "anticipation". The implied volatility of a stock that is expected to move significantly by a fixed time in the future such as an earnings announcement or court verdict increases and options on this stock become more expensive. When the event is announced, it hits the wires, any extra cost incurred from anticipation of these events will disappear completely. This is why volatility crunch is so common. Options traders who attempt to swing trade stocks after earnings releases lose money. Volatility crunch can lead you to lose money. This is because the stock may move in a predictable direction.

If you are looking to swing trade with options, then you should consider a more sophisticated strategy to speculating on high-volatility events or stocks. It is also important to be able select stocks that move before the effects time decay takes its toll.

Bid - Ask Spread

If the options have not been heavily traded, their bid ask spread can be substantially higher than that of the underlying stock. An excessive bid ask spread can cause significant upfront losses, especially for options that are not very expensive. It is important to use options trading with a tight ask spread to ensure liquidity.

Option trading can be extremely profitable and rewarding when you think about all the points and choose your options well.

Chapter 11: Market Volatility & Market Expectation

Volatility (or the tendency to fluctuate) is a common occurrence in domestic markets. However, it can be detrimental to your profits in foreign markets. What factors impact the currency's value on the foreign exchange market. Are there ways to manage this?

Devaluation & revaluation

As we have already mentioned, devaluation refers the deliberate decrease in the value a currency relative the other currencies. For example, if a U.S. currency is worth ten dollars in a foreign currency and it is then devalued ten percent, the U.S. currency is now equal to only nine of the foreign currency. Due to the lower exchange rate, foreign currency purchases are more expensive than those that trade in U.S. dollar. The exchange rate is also lower, so goods purchased overseas are more affordable for U.S. traders.

Another possible value change is the opposite, which can increase the value the foreign currency. This is called revaluation.

Although it might appear that intentionally changing the value a nation's currency could be considered fraud, or as a move in order to gain an unfair advantage by al-lowing foreign products to sell more cheaply and increasing their export value, there are rules that protect against manipulation of exchange rates. This is what the IMF (International Monetary Fund), charter does to prohibit such actions and enforce this policy.

There are several ways that you can profit off devaluations and/or revaluations. These will be discussed later.

What happens when a foreign currency's worth changes due to market fluctuations? What effect does devaluations and revaluations of foreign currencies have on the stock exchange?

Write-up and Depreciation

A car's lifespan can be extended by depreciation. When you take a new car off the lot the value is almost half. This is a huge loss of value. But, the car will lose value slowly over the next few year. Depreciation can also be described as this.

Currency appreciation or depreciation can be described as changes in currency value driven by market forces instead of government mandates. The Russian Central Bank, for instance, announced the devaluation the ruble to repay loans in 1998. The current exchange rate was six rubles to the dollar. It would increase over time to 9.5rubles per dollar. This is a 34% reduction.

The change was accompanied by panic in the once communist nation. Many Russians chose to sell their securities prior to maturity because the ruble's value fell. After the announcement, the Russian ruble saw a remarkable 25% drop in value within a single day.

In the 1920s, the U.S. stock exchange crashed and the same type of crisis was experienced. National panic set in at that point. People rushed to banks to withdraw cash that was not available or to trade stock options and securities that were not due. People ran to the bank and caused the crash, rather than escaping from it. Sociology refers to this phenomenon as a "self-fulfilling prophecy." People believed there would be a crisis even though there was none. It was only because of their actions that a crisis occurred in the aftermath. A "bank run" is a similar event in economics.

But, the flip side is that an excessive appreciation could lead to a country experiencing harmful inflation. Currency valuation can reduce inflation but it is inevitable.

You can also appreciate a car. Old cars are often restored to their original beauty by men. The vehicle's value will be greatly increased by this.

The market volatility and constantly changing currency exchange rates can create market risk. Daily loss could result from fluctuations in securities prices. As this type of risk will always impact investments, there is no way to diversify it. You can offset some of the risk by choosing investments that are safer and more protected.

Further chapters will cover long and brief positions, short selling and stop orders. These are all ways to protect your investments against serious losses. You have the option to pre-set your sell or buy price for a commodity. Additionally, you can use pre-set levels of order to place orders.

But you shouldn't be under any illusions that you can eliminate every risk factor in the market. There will always be a bubble above your head that is just waiting to burst. All it takes to burst a bubble is a small pinprick.

You should always be cautious. As you all know, being actively involved in the stock market can be dangerous and exciting.

The next chapter will help to remind you to be realistic when trading on the stock market. It will also explain how to balance your risk with reality and make sure that your It is balanced with your I.

Chapter 12: Socially Conscious Investments And The Law Of Abundance

It is essential to know that you have the divine right to live in abundance. People who are aware of excess tend to be ecologically conscious. Even those who are able to harmonize in universal law with Nature strive to include an abundance of ideas and values in all aspects of their lives.

Being more educated will help us understand that capital can be a seed. We also have to take responsibility for where our seeds are planted. Financial opportunities should only be considered if they are compatible with our values and lifestyles.

This century is more sustainable than ever. Public Funds are investment of this type. Social Funds appeared on Wall Street in 1971 and have been growing ever since. It was not clear that such funds could raise money years earlier. However, socially responsible innovation has proven profitable and is becoming increasingly possible with the advancement of technology and growing interest in the eras of spirituality and environmental consciousness.

From investing in solar panels to buying fuel-efficient automobiles, the green lifestyle has never been more appealing. Due to the increasing visibility of environmental consciousness, one isn't branded as a crazy tree-hugger with too little time. Instead, prominent artists, well-known politicians, as well as altruist industry owners, championed Planet Earth.

Affluence and awareness have begun to take root in many. As a result, more conscious, ecological, holistic people are becoming more concerned about the crimes they can finance using their money. People who had previously invested in businesses responsible for destruction of the Earth (i.e. alcohol, tobacco) or in abuses of their people (cruel labor), are now aware of their investments and more mindful about their past investments. People who live a balanced, green, conscious lifestyle are shocked at how much their dollars go to support situations that do not reflect their personal values.

The Social Investment Forum estimates that an environmental-friendly organization consisting of such intellectual investors estimates that 10% of all investment is made on social values. It now includes 151 mutual fund records with socially conscious assets greater than $148 million. This impressive growth is from the modest, but notable beginnings.

People who are more socially conscious and environmentalists get the highest return. They can be sure that their money is not harmful to Nature, its people, or the wider community. Both types of buyers see the big picture and get the most out of the final product.

Many people aren't confident in trading their traditional securities to socially-conscious funds. You don't have to beat yourself. Start quickly. Start slowly. Use traditional investment proceeds for socially conscious projects.

Becoming an angel investor in Carbon Angel. These worthwhile efforts can be felt in the long-term by supporting start ups and conscious environmental organizations.

Separately invest to support social change. Engage and mobilize supporters of groups that push Congresses for "greener" laws.

Diversify your investment portfolio with more progressive funds rather than traditional ones.

Spirituality and morality are two sides of the same coin. Nature will take care for you if it is taken care of. It is never too late if you are interested in exploring theological and fundamental laws that will allow you to live the life you dream of. Accepting the natural laws of Nature will lead you to a life that is more spiritually and financially fulfilling.

Impact Investing

These funds require contributions from organizations, businesses, or trusts in order to create a tangible and positive social or environment benefit with a safe return on investment. These are generally "for profit" businesses that do not support philanthropic and social causes. Their goal is for a more sustainable society, where all people can have equal access and enjoy the same opportunities in all areas.

Impact investments use a strategy to build (generally at the market rates) intangible or tangible financial assets intentionally, where economic value is not compromised in favor of societal value. Social impact financing assets consist of equity or bonds contributions greater than $1000 that do not offer an alternative route to ordinary companies.

Effect Social venture capital contributions should come from individuals who are economically conscious and big corporations, DFIs and pension funds. They can be directed to other activities. It can mobilise trillions in private capitals and help solve complex problems like child malnutrition, preservation and integration of the environment, aging population, long-term unemployment and agriculture. Because there is so much at stake, everyone involved must work together to make the most of it.

Social Investment Bonds or SIBs (Social Performance Checks) are two examples of innovative ways to use funds. Other funding options include microfinance loans, networks and investing channels, as well as web-based investment channels and networks.

JPMorgan Chase was the first to invest in social finance in Kenya's Wilmar Flora through USAID and Bill and Melinda Gates Foundation. The African Agricultural Capital Fund will provide funding for the African Agricultural Capital Fund. This fund will export and supply flowers with at least 2,50000 smallholder farming communities. It is just one example of the portfolio.

Aavishkar & Acumen are among the many Indian organizations engaged in impact activities related to education, Aavishkar and agriculture. Karadi Road (Aavishkar) and Karadi Road use a special language learning approach to help school children become fluent in their languages. Additionally, many people living in poverty have access, through the Vatsalya Hospitals, to world-class medicine at extremely affordable rates. Acumen has invested in renewable energy with funding from IDEO.org, DOW, and other companies to fund the solar lightmaker d.light. This intervention resulted is unit sales exceeding 500,000 per monthly.

These are only a few examples if impact investments, and their positive, far reaching impact, that can change people's course.

Investment impact measurement forms an integral part. To evaluate themselves, organizations currently use three interdependent impact metrics. PULSE is a combination of GIIRS, IRIS and PULSE. IRIS employs a number common concepts by all stakeholders for describing results. PULSE is a tool to handle specific portfolios of business. GIIRS is a framework that measures impacts as well as a research platform for analyzing businesses on a societal and environmental basis.

This degrading work is an ongoing one, whose high waters seem unbeatable. The amalgamation and advancement of money, technology, and industry to benefit the human race seems to be getting old!

Why is it important to invest ethically?

There are many issues that face the society in which they live. However, the current state and climate of the global economy are of great concern to us. They are also seen in the news. Recent coverage of the economy has been extensive. This is because economists have been expecting a troubling time as the economy for the majority are rapid.

In recent years, much has been written about the problem of global warming. It was announced that the world's population will soon reach 7 billion. The effects of this increase on the planet's natural capital must be addressed in the coming years. This cumulative environmental effect for car owners worldwide has been caused by many causes, including rising greenhouse gasses.

The impact of trees is enormous today. Because trees are essential for the environment, they're being processed at an alarming rate to satisfy the demands from the global woodworking industry. Investing in something positive not only benefits the community but also helps you long term.

How does it work?

Perhaps you've heard the expressions 'responsible,' or a 'socially responsible investor' before. They are sometimes called 'eco' or ethical' but mean the exact same thing. Ethical and green investments are investments that have the impact of investing in order to achieve a financial return on society and the planet. This particular venture requires that you consider the impact on social and environmental values.

An ethical investment is an investment that aims to maximize both financial gain and social welfare. This promotes diversity's environmentally-friendly aspect. These contributions include concern for environmental and social concerns as part of the development or operation equity portfolios.

Will you ethically and responsibly invest?

As you get older, taking care of your money is crucial for your financial future. Financial institutions like banks, brokerages, insurance companies and pension funds have more capital available to lend and spend. This process is performed on your behalf, even if it is your insurance, savings or loan.

It is a good choice to choose green and sustainable products. It will not only work for your wallet, but will also make a difference in the world and help the environment. It makes sense to make ethical financial choices and do your best to help the environment. You can only make money and have an impact on society by choosing to spend ethically and responsibly.

The majority of businesses believe that profit should be increased in all possible ways. People are willing to accept greater financial returns as a priority. But not at any price. A profit can be made by ethical investments that adhere to many of the same principles as before. These businesses are not less competitive, but more responsible corporate owners. You can both earn dividends and save money by getting your investments right the first go.

These are worth considering for a while.

You may not have known about ethically investing. This project could be beneficial in many ways. It will protect your life and help to improve the world.

Forecasting ethical and environmentally-sound spending can be a more efficient medium-term to long-term plan. There are many people who will make money by making others miserable. Individuals, NGOs, corporations and other entities should all take advantage the ethical investment approach. Many environmentally-conscious activities contribute to the beneficial facets of corporate life. These actions promote respect for culture as well the environment.

The investment problems will cause a crisis. The capital market recycles the thousands of people's pensions, savings and insurance contributions. This capital is then used in businesses to maximize profits at all rates. It's your money and your life. What can you do to ensure your financial future is not ruined by your own money? Your personal investment could be affected by the economy's drive to "make rich quick".

This is because they are incompatible with all regulations for economic development that operate within the borders of natural capital.

You have the option of social and ethical investment. This is a wonderful choice because it allows you not to be associated with companies that are hostile to your interests. It is possible to engage in people who are spiritual and reflect your moral standing. If you choose to invest ethically, it will be a positive contribution to the environment and the overall climate. It reduces our carbon footprint and protects the rainforest. Responsible investing helps you save money and help the world improve continuously.

Socially Responsible Investment - Doing Good and Doing Well

What is the best way to be a socially responsible investor and an equally good investor? Is it reasonable to consider the effects of investment products or businesses on society? Socially responsible investments allow individuals to do good in their local (and worldwide) communities and make money. Although these competing desires may seem unachievable to some people, financially responsible companies do have money. Many investment instruments can be used to satisfy the wishes of people who wish to access the market without having to compromise their consciences.

Socially Responsible Investment History, (SRI), has not become a trendy trend. In the 18th, 19th and 20th centuries, Quakers opposed selling slavery for religious reasons. John Wesley (1703-1791), a pioneer in SRI adoption, described his core ideas of social spending in his sermon on "Capital Use". Don't hurt your neighbor with your business activities. John Wesley (the founder of Methodism) preached against any business that might harm workers' health and safety in his sermon.

Many civil and political movements were formed over the 20th Century through boycotts and peaceful demonstrations against businesses that support racism, discrimination, and use weapons of war. As labor unions grew in strength, they used the enormous economic impact of their large numbers to invest pensions in medical facilities and housing for trade unions.

Apartheid Resistance Many large institutions from around the US and world have stayed away from South African apartheid investments since the 1970s. South Africa has been the subject of news stories about the persecuting of Black and non-White citizens. Cities, governments, businesses and educational institutions have all had to cease operations with South Africa. The pressure was so intense that 75% South African employers formed a charter calling for an end to apartheid.

In order to be encouraged and directed in socially responsible investment (SRI), one does not need to belong to a Church or trade organization in the 21st century. There are many investment clubs, mutual funds, blogs, directories and micro-loan agents that support a wide variety of social and politically important causes.

* SocialFunds.com contains over 10000 pages with information on SRI mutual funds, group contributions and market analysis. They also provide daily reports on social investments.

* The Calvert Foundation portfolio is an investment in a dynamic group of high impact organizations. Their goals include affordable housing, micro-finance and Fair Trade coffee. They also support the growth of small enterprises and vital community services, such as charters and nursery.

* The GreenMoney Report supports and facilitates understanding business, finances, customer products, in and online financially, as well as environmentally conscious journals.

* Ethical Investment offers investment resources for people who are interested in ethical investing, including mutual funds. The

site also has an interesting report that explains why Monsanto will never be spent.

* Network of Renewable Funds, Inc. Profiles of socially responsible products and services companies, as well SRI holdings, with mutual funds for investors, customers, businesses, and job-seekers.

* Portfolio 21 invests into businesses that produce superior goods, use renewable materials, and develop efficient methods of production.

* Winslow is a well-respected leader in renewable innovation within this fast-growing sector.

* Prosperous peer–to-peer lending that allows people and organizations to share their wealth.

* Zopa is a social finance company that was founded in 2009.

* Modest Needs (an award-winning public charity) works to stop poverty from starting

with low-income people who have been neglected by traditional philanthropy.

What Is Socially Responsible Investment?

It is the financing of renewable technology and businesses. This applies to businesses that have a proven track record in increasing their environmental impacts as well as businesses providing renewable energy solutions such solar and wind power. Green investors would also refrain from investing in companies with negative environmental effects. Socially responsible investing emphasizes businesses that produce social and environmental value. It excludes corporations that have an adverse effect on society. These are examples of social responsibility. Companies that make a significant contribution to charitable causes or have minimal environmental impacts are two examples. Environmentally conscious spending includes the abstention of other sectors like alcohol, cigarettes, defense and others.

There are six main types of spending that are socially conscious in 2010.

1 Continued technical drive.

2011 will be the same as 2011, when technology was an integral part of social innovation foundations. This is the technology advancement that will enable the planet's prosperity to increase, from electricity to food shortage. The underlying trend for the development of strong foundations in socially responsible investments portfolios will be the advancement of technology and subsequently human productivity.

2 Renewable electricity sources

In the quest for cost-effective renewable energy technologies, socially responsible enterprises and investors continue to push renewable energies forward. Shell will, for instance, increase its investment in renewable technology such as wind, sun, and solar energy and invest in sustainable fuels for the next generation. These biofuels will not increase food costs or cause deforestation. The technology will mature and a new form of economically efficient renewable energy will be developed. As more energy sources become sustainable, green investments will grow.

3. Tide change for all businesses

As human rights, corporate governance, and environmental campaigns move into the mainstream market spotlights, both businesses and individuals must be open to shifting perspectives and held accountable for their corporate governance practices. Companies have to keep up with the evolving trend because of the rising influence and strength of social investments dollars. This makes them $1 out every five dollars in managed investment funds. Walmart, the flagship retail company, is one example. It recently released their first sustainable reports and began offering organic products and sustainable agriculture products in its stores.

4 International steps towards warming

With the launch of the Climate Change Fund, global warming policies will continue to drive the growth in socially responsible investments. It is up to companies to respond to new demands from the political world as well as researchers. There are also large profits to make. Innovest strategic quality advisors released a study called "Carbon Beta" that showed that businesses who capitalized on the potential for climate change have made more than their counterparts. This importance will only continue to grow with government measures aiming at tighter pollution standards that favor the environmentally-conscious stocks aimed at addressing the environmental crisis.

5 Going Black

Sustainability screening is important because of the emphasis placed on socially responsible investments. It is expected that the global investment market will introduce new "financially effective" instruments in 2011. As the market recognizes renewable investing more widely and is being covered by media, there will be a rise in demand for such investment companies. With the opening of numerous managed and unregulated renewable funds that are focused on environmentally friendly businesses and projects, there will be a strong demand for investment in renewables in the finance sector in 2010.

Chapter 13: Advantages Of Index Funds

All types of investing have their advantages. Index funds are no different. Index funds offer many advantages. In fact, I won't be covering them all here. One reason for this is that index funds can be beneficial to different people. Index funds are becoming a more popular type of investing. This means that index funds are being increasingly researched by investors every day.

Passive Management

As I stated previously, you can choose to manage your investing passively or actively. There are two main differences between them. Those who actively manage investments keep an eye on the market in order to ensure their investment beats the market. Active investors regularly check on their investments.

Passive investors tend focus on their investments only quarterly or annually.

Passive investors may not be as concerned about their returns. However, this is a result of the type investments they made. Many investors consider it a major benefit to be able to manage their investment portfolio passively. This allows them more time to enjoy their lives and less stress. Index funds are a popular choice for investors.

Index funds are passive investments. This is because there is no managing involved. All that is required is to ensure that the performance between the indexes is as consistent as possible. Because the index funds are so easy to manage, investors can be able focus on factors that could help them become better investors. Instead of spending their time managing their investments, they can concentrate on learning as much as possible about the market.

Financial Advantages

Experienced investors will tell you to not be too focused on the amount of money that you will make when investing. This can lead to people thinking irrationally about the decisions they make and can quickly lead them to develop psychological biases. This is more common among active fund investors because they constantly monitor their funds. Additionally, many active funds charge higher fees that index funds.

If funds charge low fees, index fund investors will see higher returns. Index funds' low fees are due to the fact that they are passive funds, which are easy to manage and operate. Fees are lower for index funds and may be waived for some funds. Not all investments will charge commission fees. With enough research, it is easy to find an index fund with low fees but high returns.

Steady Growth with Low Risk

An additional advantage of index funds is the fact that they can be used long-term to help you invest. Stocks and bonds are popular investments because they are considered low-risk. This allows people to save over time. So if you want to make money quickly and are interested in investing, this is not the way to go. If you are in your 30s, and you want to increase retirement income, you can look into which types of index funds may be right for you.

You can also find index funds with diversity. This means you could have one investment lose and another invest the difference. Index investing is a way to make your losses equal with your gains. You will still be able to see a return on other investments.

Diversification can be an advantage

Diversification is both a positive and negative aspect of the market. However, in this chapter we will only focus on diversification as an advantage. Diversification refers to the ability to have multiple investments in your portfolio. This is the goal of any market investor. Because index funds typically have a high level of market diversity, it makes this easy. The index's diversity means that your investments are more protected than if they were just individual stocks, bonds, and other types of investments.

Low Turnover

Ideal is to have low turnover with your investments. If you have a high turnover, you'll end up paying more for management and maintenance fees. This could reduce the return on your investments. Index funds tend to have lower turnovers so there is less to worry about. You won't be affected by the turnover. You can see an example: If your index contains 100 stocks and you observe that 20 of them have moved over in the last year, your turnover rate is 20%. This is a low rate to invest in.

A lower level of psychological bias

The psychology involved in investing is something that people often don't know. Psychology is the study the human mind and behavior. When you invest, you often use psychology. Investors can resort to psychological bias in almost any decision they make unless they are very careful. Psychological bias is a problem in decision making because it causes people's to think in an unrational way. There are several types of psychological biases that investors frequently use. These are just a few of the forms.

There are two types of psychological bias that can be related: regret and anchoring. Both are related to holding on to past mistakes, making it harder to make the right decisions for the future. Investors regret past decisions and allow them to impact their current decisions. Anchoring is similar. Investors allow their past choices to impact their present decisions. Instead of allowing them to make the right decisions now, they cling to those past decisions. This leaves them unable to understand the market. Some investors become paranoid about making the same mistakes again, and they start to overthink their choices or allow their emotions control.

One form psychological bias centers on the risks that investors take when they consider diversification. Many investors believe that diversifying your portfolio is beneficial long-term. Investors can fall into the psychological bias that mental accounting creates, believing they have a more balanced portfolio than they actually are. This is when investors are willing to take risks in a particular market area but not in others. Diversifying your portfolio means you need to invest in many areas of the market.

Narrow framing, a psychological bias that is common in investors at the beginning, is another. This happens when an investor makes a decision without considering the implications for their entire portfolio. They will look at how the decision will affect everything around them. They don't take into account all parts of their portfolio.

I mentioned earlier that it is important to stay positive and feel confident when investing in the markets. It is also important to keep up-to-date with the competition. If you are a positive person, it is easy to get caught up in the trap of watching other investors fail within the market. This psychological bias is also known as irrational optimism.

Many new investors also fall prey to the psychological bias known as herding. This is easy to do for new investors because it involves following other investors and making the same decisions. This can be problematic because you're not focusing on what is best and your portfolio. You also don't understand why another investor makes these decisions. You may find it helpful to consult your broker/trusted advisor. However, you want to be sure that you fully understand what you are doing and how it will affect your investing career.

Index funds are passive investments so you won't be affected by psychological bias. Index funds are easier than other investments. They are also easier to learn and understand. It is easy to purchase, maintain and track your expected returns. The ease of index funds is known to take a lot stress and worry out investing. This makes it easier for you to manage your emotions. Many times, emotional biases are rooted in psychological factors. As an example, if your past decisions are held on to, you may become anxious and stressed about your future choices. These emotions can lead one to regretting or anchoring.

There are fewer psychological worries

When you invest in index fund, there are many things that can help to ease your mind. Index funds are passively managed. This is especially helpful for people with busy lifestyles. Index funds can be managed more easily than other funds.

Index funds are passive funds, so you don't have to devote a lot time to managing them. Instead, you can devote a few hour per week to managing the funds. The rest of your life will be taken over by index funds. As you don't have to spend as many hours on the selling and buying side of investing, you can dedicate more time to research or other areas. This is beneficial in many different ways. You will be informed about any updates regarding index fund investing. It will also help make you more consistent and confident and allow you to work on the best strategies that suit your lifestyle.

Also, index fund investment can help reduce stress. People can feel stressed when investing for a variety of reasons. This can lead to more problems such as anxiety and losing control of your emotions. Index investing can help reduce your anxiety and improve your mood. You will find your mind feels calmer and more relaxed due to index investing's passive nature. This will help your mind feel more relaxed and calm.

Great for Beginners

Index funds offer another advantage: they can be used as a good starting point for new investors. This is due to the ease of index funds being passive investments. The second reason is that they can be managed easily, passively, so beginners can take their own time learning about the market and investing. This also helps beginners, as they are less likely for their emotions to dictate how they make decisions.

Index investing is a great way for investors who have never invested before to get a feel for the world of investing. You don't need to begin investing in the stock market as soon as you are experienced. Index funds can be used to help you start investing and you can keep in touch your advisor. Expert investors feel that this is one way that you can gain knowledge about the market. The best way to learn about investing is while you're actually doing it. It gives you an easier, more hands-on approach which not only helps you retain what you have learned but also makes it clearer. As our brains only have so many new information to retain, we learn best when we are actively learning.

Index Funds are simple to use

An index fund is transparent and there are no hidden charges. Index funds have an underlying index benchmark which allows investors to see the index's past history.

Brokers are limited in their risk

Although it is important to keep up-to date with what's happening with your investments and to avoid any potential risks, index funds are more reliable than brokers. The risk of losing money is higher if funds are actively managed. This is because the broker is more likely making costly mistakes. But, if your decision is to invest in index fund, it's less likely as these investments are passive. You often follow the "buy and hold" strategy. Both you and your broker want to stay informed, but you are free to let go of some of the responsibilities.

Index Funds Are Silent Competitors

It is not difficult to see that the market is very competitive. Many people believe that being competitive is essential to success in the stock market. People who don't often win in any type of competition are more comfortable with investing in CDs. Retirement accounts, bonds and high-interest savings account than the stock markets. Passive index funds could be for you if your competitive nature is not a problem but you don't like actively managed funds.

While index funds remain competitive on the market, they are less prominent than their silent counterparts. Index funds aim to offer you the highest rate of return over a prolonged period of time. While there is still competition for index funds to ensure you get the best possible return, their growth is slower than that of other stocks.

They can help you to build your portfolio

Index funds are passive. Because they require less maintenance, this is a major advantage. It can help build your portfolio. As you watch your savings grow through index funds, you can still learn about investing. After you feel more at ease, you can explore other types and investments to add to your portfolio. This will help you concentrate on finding low-cost investments as well as allow you to spend time researching the best stocks to diversify you portfolio.

There's very little maintenance

You don't have to do much maintenance when it comes to index funds. Index funds are not as active managed investments. You can still clean up your portfolio frequently and keep track of market news, but they won't require you to do as much maintenance. While it's important to not forget your investments, you can purchase them and then let your savings grow while you worry less about what you should do next. Index funds are often used to help people secure financial security in retirement and provide large returns.

Index Funds Outperform Other Funds

You have two options when it comes to investing in funds. Index funds are passive. This means they don't require any maintenance during their time in your portfolio. Index funds often outperform actively managed ones. Although there aren't many strong reasons why this happens, Warren Buffett (and John Bogle) who were strong advocates of index funds claim that it is because you buy the investment, then hold it for as much time as possible. Both of these millionaires employed the buy and keep strategy. They are two of the most prominent examples of how index funds can help increase wealth, over actively managed funds. According to statistics, there's a 75% chance that investing in index funds will result in a higher rate of return than if it was invested elsewhere.

You know that you are not the only one

When they first invest, many investors worry about the performance and health of their portfolios. You don't need to worry about it if you invest in index stock. You can also see how index funds of other investors are doing. You will know that if the stock of another person is doing well, your stock should be doing similarly. On the flip side, if your stock is beginning to perform poorly you will know that it is doing well.

You can feel calmer knowing that you're not alone can help reduce psychological anxiety and improve your ability to control your emotions. Even if you feel that one of the stocks you own is not performing as it should, the problem may not be your fault. The stock belongs to everyone. This can provide investors with the knowledge and confidence they need to grow. This is just one reason index investing is so popular with beginners.

Chapter 14: Scalping Guide

"Volatility is most high at turning points. It decreases as a trend becomes established."

George Soros

Scalping may be the best option for you if your trading needs are short-term. Scalping, unlike day trading which involves placing trades in a single trading day and holding them until the end of that trading day, is shorter. Scalping is a trade that you do multiple times in a day. This helps you make every penny for the day.

Many people are now jumping on the day trading bandwagon. You're right! But what if your trading needs are shorter and simpler than day trading. If you're looking to make small profits, or just catch the little price fluctuations in the market several times per day, then this is the right option for you. What if the game is your passion and you want to see the screen every single minute?

Don't worry about trying to do the same thing as other traders. The most important thing is to choose the trading style that you like. This is where scalping may work well for you. Scalping might not be the best option for you if your goal is to become a successful position trader.

Scalping Basics

Remember that the trading style you choose is determined by who you are. You are not a follower of the crowd. You will do what is best for your trading style and approach. Position traders are expected to have a long-term perspective on assets. Your system might work well when you move to scalping trading.

A day trader can however use scalping multiple times a day. Day trading typically involves holding positions on average for thirty minutes. Scalping involves trading positions that last from seconds to five minutes. This is why scalpers love looking at five-minute stock chart charts. It makes it easier to make profitable scalping decisions.

Scalper can't wait to trade for more than a few days. He or she is an active trader looking for the best possible profit in the markets in the shortest time. In other words, a scalper trades more often than all other traders during a trading session. Scalping is a skill that can be learned.

Investopedia defines "scalping" as "a trading technique that focuses in making small profit from price changes. This is usually done after a trade is executed. Scalping requires that traders have a defined exit strategy. One large loss can wipe out the small gains they worked so hard to achieve. This strategy must be well-planned and have the tools needed to succeed, including a livefeed and direct access broker.

You should know these two things. One, scalping does not focus on profiting from large price movements. Two, seasoned scalers do not care about massive price changes. Scalper make trading easy by executing profitable trades and making profits.

Types of Scalping

Scalp trades are influenced by three key factors: pricing, volatility, and volume. Before you begin to use scalping, learn as much as you can about the essential elements of scalping. They have an impact on scalping and can also be used to create scalping options that will make you successful in the financial marketplace.

"Less Volatile security" Approach

This type of scalping targets less volatile stocks and no price changes. They also have high trading volumes. Scalpers will trade profitably once there is high trading volume. This type of scalping can be called "market-making".

This strategy is used by a scalper who is trying to bet on "market makers". He/she posts simultaneously a bid for the financial instrument and an offer. To quickly make profit in the market, you will use the price difference between your offer and the bid.

Success depends on your ability to analyse the stock's movement and volume.

"Highly Volatile Security."

A trading strategy that is compatible with volatility can be used when a stock or financial instrument moves quickly. Scalp trading can be a great option when the market is volatile as pricing changes quickly.

This strategy involves buying large numbers of shares and placing a wager against price movement. You will profit if the stock price moves slightly. It must be liquid. Before you can trade, you should evaluate the market and time it well. The goal is to wait for small movements to make a profit.

"Close at Entry" Approach

You use the same or similar trading strategies as in the second trading approach. To make money, you wait for prices to drop a little. However, here you are more focused upon your exit. You can close the trade once the exit strategy has been met.

You will need to use this method to create and analyze an exit strategy. This will allow you both to profit from your scalp and minimize losses from market reversals. Ideal risk/reward ratios for this type of trade are 1:1.

Trading Psychology for Scalpers

Scalper believes that it is simpler to make money from small price movements in the market than waiting for large price swings to make a profit. The small profits that scalpers accumulate are what gives them an edge over long-term traders, such as position traders.

It is important to know how to think, act, and behave in order for you to be a successful scalper. If you don't have a specific way of thinking, behaving and acting, you might give up before you achieve success. No matter what type of financial instrument or scalping strategy you use, here are three behavioral and psychological patterns you must possess.

Consistency

Scalping might seem simple from the outside. But if your trading system is not followed consistently, it will be difficult to scale. Scalper trades are made every few minutes. You must plan and organize your trading to avoid mistakes. You'll only end up wasting your trading capital on useless items if you don't.

Discipline

The decision-making process of a scalper differs from that of a swing or day trader. To be successful you need to work hard. Once you've made a decision about a trade, there is no time for feeling or rehearsing. To quickly enter or exit trades, you will need to learn how to make quick decisions.

Flexible

You shouldn't be too hard on yourself or rigid about your trading plan and system. But you also need to be flexible. Flexibility is important to adjust to market changes, even if they aren't covered in your trading plans.

Don't be discouraged if a trade doesn't go according to plan. Just exit the market and move onto the next one.

Commitment for research

For position traders, it takes a lot of research. But for scalpers, it is much more. When scalping, you have to be able to place more trades in a given day. You need to do your research on all types of securities and how they are related before you can start scalping. Doing so will ensure that your trades are constructed well and you have the best chance of being successful.

Chapter 15: Retaining And Managing Your Tenants

Its one thing managing your rental property with care, but it's quite another to maintain your tenants. You can't just ensure you follow the law, and provide the best services to retain your tenants. Is it important to retain your tenants? Many landlords think that letting a tenant leave is not something to worry about, especially when they have other tenants available. Tenants that stay with you for a significant amount of time are a great way to get the most out of your property. We'll be discussing the many benefits of retaining tenants, as well as the ways you can ensure that your tenants stay for the long-term.

Benefits of having Long-Term Tenants

Property management is all about your tenants. Your failure to retain tenants is your first sign that your property manager is doing a poor job. Even if you're doing things right, you might still have trouble keeping long-term renters. To retain your tenants, you need to understand the benefits of long-term renters. The following are some of the benefits that long-term tenants can enjoy:

Reduced void periods

Long-term tenants can reduce the time period between when the property is declared vacant and when the unit is occupied. It is possible that a tenant may decide to leave your house during the month. However, you might not be able or able to find a new tenant for the same unit until after a few months. This should be considered if you have rental properties that are located in low-demand areas. Because people are constantly searching for apartments in New York, it is possible to have short periods of void if you own property in that city. However, those who live in more populated cities or towns might have to wait several weeks before a new tenant is found. In the long-term, these void periods could be detrimental to your income.

There are no regular 'tenant finding' fees

Searching for tenants can be costly. We have seen that erecting a signboard outside your vacant property does not work in modern times. It may be necessary to list your property on several real-estate listing sites. Some of these sites can charge fees. The best way to avoid paying these fees is to have long-term tenants. You don't have to pay agents to find new tenants.

Expectations shared understanding

Tenants are the same as colleagues or friends at work. A friend who has been around for a long time will be able to tell you what to do and where you should go to maintain your friendship. The same goes for long-term tenants. Lack of understanding of the client's needs is one reason property managers fail. Being with your tenants for a longer period of time will help you understand the needs and desires of your tenants. The more time you spend with your tenant, you will get to know their personalities. Understanding a person is better than starting a relationship with a stranger. You can manage your expectations by retaining as many tenants possible.

It lowers the chances of getting an unwanted tenant

If there is one tenant that you do not want, managing the property could become a nightmare. As we have already stated, different people have different lives and personalities. Your tenants might have a life style that is totally different to yours. This may make your job much more difficult than you had hoped. It is better to keep your tenants around for longer than you think.

Reduced wear and tear during "moveins" and "moveouts".

You could be liable for serious damages from the moving process. It is better to keep tenants in the property for a longer period of time than to have to deal continuously with damage and repair. Many times, constant moving causes damage to the windowpanes or door handles and locks. Retaining tenants for a prolonged period can prevent these damages and losses.

It is more likely that a long-term tenant will take good care of the property.

Another benefit of long-term tenants being tenants is their property care. If you are planning to stay for a while, you will treat the property as if it was your own. For tenants who intend on staying for a while, the same principle applies. Watching how they care for the apartment can tell you if they are long-term-minded.

Common Mistakes Property owners Make That Can Cost Tenants Their Property

Common mistakes property owners make can often result in losing key tenants. To ensure that your tenants stay with us for as long time as possible, it is essential to avoid these common mistakes. It is crucial for tenants to understand the difference between property management & social interactions. Property managers are often confused because there are so many variables involved in property management. Every property should be viewed as a business entity and a service provision entity. As such, the property manager should be able to manage finances and offer services to tenants.

Tenants can end up separating from their landlords by trying to balance all aspects of property management. Below are some mistakes that property managers can make to lose tenants.

Prolonging conflict

It's normal for tenants to have disputes with the property manager. You will determine whether your tenants are retained or not by how you handle these disputes.

You can approach disputes with professionalism. Always follow the law in resolving any dispute. In making your decisions, you should look at your property laws and take into account the laws of both the state and local governments. It is best to avoid court proceedings if you want your tenants to stay. It is possible to reach an amicable settlement. In some cases, it may be necessary to reach a compromise to ensure that the issue is resolved quickly. But, you should not compromise when matters are serious and infringe upon the rights or property of other tenants. The more you delay in resolving any issue, the worse your relationship with your tenant.

Failure to set tenant rules

Instead of spending too many hours trying to resolve conflict, you can try to prevent conflicts from ever occurring. The lack of clear guidelines and rules are often the root cause of conflicts in rental properties. Be patient when creating your property rules. Do not copy and paste other property manager's laws. Take the time to learn about the unique challenges facing your property, and then create rules that promote harmony in the property.

Your property rules should not be used to infringe upon your tenants' rights or freedoms. Your property rules should not be used to limit the rights and freedoms of tenants. As an example, while all tenants should have the freedom to express their opinions, they shouldn't be a nuisance for their neighbors. Clearly stating what tenants may and cannot do will reduce conflicts. Finding the right tenants will allow you to settle your disputes, as long as they agree to abide with your property rules.

Don't be too friendly to your renters

We have already talked about maintaining a good working relationship with your tenants. It is crucial to keep in touch with your tenants and remain on good terms. It is important to maintain a positive relationship with your tenants. A friendly relationship can be maintained through exchanging pleasantries.

It is important to distinguish between your friendships and your professional responsibilities. Being a manager of a property is not the best way to spend time with tenants. It is important that tenants see you as the landlord and not just as a friend. Friends are not good friends if you will have to question your tenants' behavior. Be careful about what you allow to happen in your relationships.

Being a "Jack of all Trades."

Owning a property can be costly. You might be tempted, if you keep finding problems with water leaks, electrical faults, etc., to fix them all yourself. Many tenants take care of all the property's requirements without consulting professionals or third parties. This can lead to financial losses, and often the loss of your tenants. Instead of trying to manage your property's problems, let professionals do so. Service providers such as plumbers, electricians, and garbage collectors should be professionals.

A property manager can also be a great way to get rid of many of the hassles that property owners face. Property managers are trained to handle customer complaints professionally. If you attempt to handle everything yourself, you'll run out of resources, delay responding to customers, and ultimately lose your tenants.

Renting units without a strategic price

Another problem that could lead to you losing tenants is the failure to correctly price your properties. In order to set the right prices for your property, it is essential that you remain in the loop.

Prices of property fluctuate according to the market. Most homeowners had reduced their property prices during the COVID-19 peak. It is important to evaluate the current situation and price your property accordingly. Renters will often move to lower-priced units if the prices you set are too high. When increasing rental prices, you must have a legitimate reason. If your property price is lower than market average, you may be able to increase it with a valid reason.

A management company that deals only with leasing is a good idea.

It is acceptable to hire a management agency to manage your rental properties. Renting a management company that focuses on leasing will cost you more than a rental agency that specializes in managing your property. You should look for companies that understand customer needs if you hire professionals to manage your properties. The company should strive to provide the best tenant service, not just get the lease signed. The wrong tenants will be found if the company is focused on the money. Property managers must be able understand your tenants' needs and offer value to them. This will ensure that your tenants are happy and stay with you for a lifetime.

Best Strategies to Retain Tenants You Already Have

Losing a tenant may seem easy but maintaining one takes effort. Making a single mistake can result in losing all your tenants. But, to ensure that you retain only one tenant for a long duration, you must do things differently. Tenants will stay with you if they feel your property is valuable and unique. It all boils down to providing excellent customer service. Here are some customer service tips to help tenants stay.

Reward good tenants

Renter's behavior can be rewarded and punished in a one-sided rental market. It is common for landlords not to pay rent on time and to punish tenants who cause damage to the rental property. Rarely will you find landlords who offer a reward to tenants for paying the rent on time, or taking care about the property. Property rules will usually outline the consequences of missed rent payments. Changes in your approach to tenants can help you retain them. It is possible to encourage your tenants not to pay rent on the due date by offering a discount instead of punishing them.

Rents must be competitive

Rent pricing is another factor that will help you keep tenants happy for years. Some landlords are greedy and raise the rent beyond market value. Even if your property is of the highest quality, it will not be a good idea to charge tenants exorbitant rent. Your customers must feel fair and treated. If they see that they are paying too much to rent a space that is more affordable, they will likely move on. For your customers to stay loyal, find out the average price of rental properties in your area. Comparisons of leasing prices can be made on Craigslist and Zillow. The comparison will give an indication of the market range that you can use to make sure your tenants don't pay too much or too little.

Tenant Feedback

Tenant feedback is also an important aspect. It is important to use every means possible to get feedback from tenants about your property, services, or the rent you charge. This will enable you to adjust your services and property in order for clients to be satisfied. There are many options for getting customer feedback. Surveys or a suggestion form could be used. If you do choose to gather tenant responses, make certain that they remain unanimous. If tenants feel the information could lead to discrimination, they will not share all of their information.

Conclusion

With this book, Stock market you will be able to learn all aspects of stocks and how it functions in the market. Because there are many sides to the stock market, it is easier to understand when you are actually in the real world. This information can help you navigate the competitive market to acquire shares and show you how you can make good decisions for your company and yourself. It is always safer to invest in the right area. You should first assess your situation before thinking about investing in stocks.

The book can help you understand the basics and then show you how to apply them in your daily life. If you are lucky enough to get stocks, however, you may lose all your investments if the market crashes. You can learn a lot from this book. Make wise decisions that positively impact your life.

www.ingramcontent.com/pod-product-compliance
Lightning Source LLC
Chambersburg PA
CBHW050404120526
44590CB00015B/1822